The A-Z G[illegible] o Teachin[illegible] in South Korea

Learn Whether South Korea is Right for You, How to Survive and How to Prosper There

Adrian Bozon

Crazy Chopstick Publications

ISBN 978-0-956796837

Published by Crazy Chopstick Publications.

enquiries@crazychopstickpublications.com

Disclaimer: The publisher does not wish to enter into disputes of the Romanized spellings of Korean words in this book. Additionally, neither the publisher nor author can be held responsible for anyone who has a bad experience teaching in Korea.

Contents

Part 2A

Part 2B

Foreword

One dull afternoon in the spring of 2002, I decided to go for a walk down to my local careers office. It was a decision which changed my life.

I did not have a specific purpose in mind when I entered the building but I soon found myself attracted to a file containing overseas jobs. I started to flick through the first few pages and saw various jobs in Western European countries. There was nothing there that inspired me but then I turned over to the next page and saw a job teaching English in Japan. This seemed a lot more appealing and captured my imagination but I continued onwards to the following page and there it was - South Korea! It instantly leaped out at me. It seemed so exciting and different.

The overview of Korea was captivating. The culture seemed fascinating. The work sounded good. The monthly pay was in Korean won and was a seven figure number. I would only have to work one month and then I would become a millionaire! I had no idea how many British Pounds or American Dollars it converted to but when I later checked, it actually worked out to be a very reasonable amount with a low cost of living and an additional month's salary at the end of the contract on top.

I researched Korea in more detail, made some enquiries and soon applied for a teaching job there. One successful telephone interview later and it was time to make the necessary preparations for departure. When I broke the news to friends and family around me there were some very surprised and shocked people! Some got their world atlas out to find out where Korea actually is. There was also some concern naturally – after all North Korea does get a lot of negative coverage in the press. Would I be safe? What about the language? How would I cope in my everyday life there without being able to speak Korean? How would I be able to teach Korean children English without speaking Korean?

It soon became clear to people around me that nothing was going to change my mind. I was going to do a one year contract and have a tremendous experience before returning home. I spent the 2002 FIFA World Cup held in South Korea and Japan as a very interested television spectator and a few months later I was on my way there. I ended up liking it so much that I spent most of the next ten years there.

I was very lucky that most of my experiences in South Korea were so positive. I enjoyed my work most of the time, became accustomed to the culture and met many great people. Many other foreigners head to Korea to teach English and have similar glowing experiences too but for a significant minority the outcome is not so positive with complaints about workplace issues often being at the forefront.

Most foreign English teachers planning to go to South Korea have to start off with one very big decision. Should they start off by teaching in a hagwon (an academy) or at a public school? Both of these have a number of good and bad points as well as numerous pitfalls to avoid. This book provides a very detailed guide to teaching at hagwons and public schools, explains some of the issues teachers may face and offers suggestions for preventing difficult situations or handling them as and when they arise.

The information provided in this book aims to serve a few key purposes. First of all, it is designed to help potential teachers decide whether South Korea is right for them or whether they might be better off investigating other countries to work in. The next important target is to help people make the right individual choice between public schools and hagwons because what is best for one person will not necessarily be right for the next. Finally, the book addresses a whole range of work situations and classroom scenarios teachers often face in South Korea.

Learn what motivates young Korean learners, what activities they like, what aspects of English they struggle with, what problems sometimes occur in the classroom and what to do about them. Discover what will be expected of you at your workplace, what information you need to establish and check for before signing a contract and why things happen at work in Korea in the way that they do. Find out whether you need to complete any kind of short teaching course or qualification prior to flying out, whether you can take your partner with you and why Korean children often have two different names and ages!

I hope this book will prepare new and inexperienced teachers as fully as possible, help them to overcome the nervous first few days and weeks in South Korea, make sense of everything which is going on around them and put them on the road to a successful and rewarding experience. It is also designed to be a guide teachers can refer back to on an ongoing basis as they encounter new situations or problems or when they want to look for fresh ways of trying to get the best out of their students.

Good luck!

Part One
Living in South Korea

An introduction to Korean life and culture

A

Annyeong-ha-say-yo (안녕하세요?)

A logical starting point to any Korean experience is learning how to say, 'Hello'. The above expression is the most commonly used greeting in Korean and when speaking to adults you will not go wrong if you use it. If you are an adult and you are talking to children, you should drop the 'ha-say-yo' part to just say, 'Annyeong' (안녕) but kids must use the longer form of, 'Annyeong-ha-say-yo' when they greet you as you are older than them and Korean language has strict rules for usage, which are dictated by age and status.*

Agreeing

One source of frustration amongst foreigners in Korea comes when they make a request to a Korean in English for something, have the other person seemingly agree by nodding their head or saying, 'Yes,' only for nothing to happen in due course. In this situation, the Korean person usually does not fully understand but is either too shy or too embarrassed to admit not

* The more formal, 'Annyeong-ha-shim-ni-kka,' (안녕하십니까? – note that it is usually written as a question) is sometimes used instead when meeting someone for the first time.

understanding.* Do not let yourself get worked up over these situations. Bear them in mind, learn from them and use additional visual aids where possible. For example, if you want your academy director to buy more markers for your classroom, go to him or her with the last marker in your hand (and perhaps even the empty box) and kindly ask him to buy some more very soon.

Airports

Incheon is the main airport in Korea and the one where most foreigners arrive at to begin their Korean experience. It is close to Seoul. It is a well-regarded airport, which has won various awards. Staff speak English well there. South Korea's second biggest city is Busan, which also has an international airport although it does not offer as many routes as Incheon. Other smaller airports include the ones at Jeju, Cheongju, Daegu, Gimpo and Gwangju. These tend to just be used for travel around Asia and trips to and from Jeju, Korea's most famous island.

---

* This is not a 'Korean problem' per se it should be acknowledged. Many people speaking a language other than their own do not like to admit failing to fully understand. I am sure most people have also experienced slightly deaf old people agreeing with them only for it to become blatantly obvious they have no idea what they have just agreed to!

Apartments

The vast majority of Korean people live in apartments. Apartments are heavily condensed in the major cities. The cost of renting or buying apartments in Seoul is extremely high. Many foreigners will be provided with an apartment to live in by their workplace while they stay in Korea.

Arirang Song

This is a popular Korean folk song, which includes regional variations and has been around for several centuries. Women often dress in hanbok (traditional Korean costume) when they sing the song.

Arirang TV

When foreigners first arrive in Korea, usually unable to speak any Korean, they may find themselves flicking television channels in the hope of finding an English speaking channel. Arirang TV provides this. It shows a wide range of programmes including news, documentaries, educational programmes and cultural shows. The channel aims to introduce viewers to aspects of Korean society and to help them understand Korea better. The channel is very pro-Korea and has sometimes come under fire from foreigners for not giving a truly accurate picture of Korea.

B

Bank Loans

It is generally extremely difficult for a foreigner to get a bank loan in Korea and those that do manage to borrow some money will normally be married to a Korean, have lived in Korea for a long time and be able to provide something major as security on the loan. Most foreigners who need extra finance should look to their home banks or even family for assistance. Korean banks are unlikely to help.

Beaches

Korea has a large number of beaches, which open for the summer months. The most popular area for beaches is Busan with Haeundae Beach being the most famous but there are lots of nice beaches elsewhere too. Korean beaches get very packed. Many Koreans go into the sea wearing their normal summer clothes rather than swimwear.

Beer

Beer is very commonly drank in Korea. Famous Korean brands include Hite and Cass. Korean beer gets mixed reviews amongst westerners. Many bars also sell some western beers although the Korean brands are usually significantly cheaper.

Blind Dates

While living in Korea, if foreigners are single and have made a good impression on Korean friends and colleagues, it is not unusual to start receiving suggestions to go on blind dates with Koreans. Blind dates (소개팅 - so-gae-ting) are very common in Korea and are a popular way to meet men or women. The mutual friend or acquaintance organizes the meeting and goes along to introduce the man and woman. Sometimes the two will then get left to it but it is also quite common for the mutual friend to stick around for the whole of the first meeting if one or both of the people are quite shy. Common meeting places include coffee shops and cinemas.

Whereas blind dates in Korea were once something of a prelude to a brisk marriage, they are much more casual now. Younger Koreans may have numerous blind dates free of any obligations, making their own judgments as to whether to meet their date again. Koreans who have reached their mid-thirties and beyond will sometimes be hoping for blind dates to progress pretty quickly towards marriage as Korea is such a marriage-orientated society but even in these cases, the people involved are almost always free to make their own choices, although there may be some strong parental pressure in the background.

Board Game Rooms

In addition to regular entertainment such as bars, coffee shops and karaoke, Korea has plenty of other places to go. One example is the board game rooms, which are scattered around although not overly large in number. People go there with one or more of their friends and choose from a fairly large selection of boards games, both Korean and western. Drinks are also available. They are an interesting, cheap alternative way to spend a couple of hours although they can sometimes become noisy and get overrun with school students.

Business Cards

Koreans often carry business cards around with them and will usually give one to someone as soon as they meet them. When getting a business card from a Korean, receive it with two hands despite its small size. Avoid cursory glances and actually look at it carefully before putting it away somewhere professional looking such as a card holder. Do not write on business cards as it is considered rude.

Foreign English teachers do not often have their own business cards made, especially if they are only planning on staying for a year or so. For those on a longer sojourn and especially foreign businesspeople as opposed to English teachers, the need to have a business card is greater. Business cards should ideally be in English on one side and translated into Korean on the other side. As status is so important in Korea, job or rank should also be included.

C

Cellphones

One of the things most foreigners want to do within the first few days of arriving is to get a cellphone. Occasionally some have spoken of difficulties in acquiring one but most do not have any problems with the assistance of a Korean colleague or friend. Calling and texting rates are very reasonable within Korea. To contact friends and relatives in other countries, using methods such as Skype on the internet or prepaid calls from landlines will prove to be much cheaper. Korean friends or colleagues should be able to assist with buying prepaid cards from Korean websites.

Changing Names

Korean women do not change their family name after marrying. Children subsequently take their father's name as their family name. On the other hand it is more common than in the west for parents to change their children's given names for various reasons.

Cherry Blossoms

One of the most distinctive signs of Korea's spring is the sight of cherry blossoms. For a few days or so, families and friends go out together in large numbers to admire and take photographs of the beautiful scenes. There are also various cherry blossom festivals around Korea at this time.

Chopsticks

Most Korean food is eaten with chopsticks so it is a good idea to make some attempt to polish one's chopstick technique before arriving in Korea. However, those who do not master the art of chopsticks before departing their own country do not need to despair. When eating out, many restaurants will have forks available. If there are no forks at the restaurant tables, attracting a waiter's attention and saying, 'Pork' (포크), which is the Korean word for 'fork', should ensure a fork is brought to you.

Christian Missionaries

It is not unusual to see Christian missionaries who have come to Korea from the west. They often learn Korean very quickly to help them in their work. Foreigners who bump into missionaries in a public place in Korea will probably find them very friendly and happy to talk.

Churches

Christianity and Buddhism are the two most common religions in South Korea. Subsequently, there is no shortage of churches. Foreigners living in large cities (especially Seoul) should not have any major problems finding English church services if they wish to attend. Churches without English services are also likely to be welcoming even if communication proves a little problematic.

Chuseok

Along with Korean New Year, Chuseok (추석) is one of the two big Korean national holidays. It is on the fifteenth day of the eighth month by the lunar calendar, which is usually in September but it occasionally falls at the beginning of October. Chuseok is a three day holiday, which sees people visit their hometowns in massive numbers. Public transport is totally packed at this time, especially vehicles heading out of Seoul at the beginning of the holiday and then heading back to Seoul at the end of the holiday. Most journeys take significantly longer than normal during this period. During this holiday, Koreans often visit the tombs of their ancestors as well as performing rituals in their homes as marks of respect to their deceased relatives. Food is also a very important part of Chuseok as large family gatherings take place.

Coffee Shops

Young Koreans love spending their free time in coffee shops despite the fairly high prices these places sometimes charge. Some open until quite late at night, with some staying open even later on Friday and Saturday nights. Staff are often young and many will have a basic grasp of English so it is usually pretty easy for foreigners to order. Some foreigners go alone and there is sometimes the possibility to meet other foreigners and perhaps build new friendships or social contacts.

Crazy!

In English, 'crazy' can be used as a way of describing someone or something very negatively and it is also frequently used for fun or when someone is joking. In Korean too, it *can* be used in a jocular context but perhaps less so than in English. When the Korean word for 'crazy' is used a non-jocular way in Korean, it is a particularly bad word and likely to offend, perhaps not translating quite literally from English to Korean. Even if you attempt to use it for humour, there are no certainties that the Korean you are talking to will realize what you are doing and misunderstandings could occur. If at all possible, it is a Korean word that should be avoided in any Korean language conversations you may have with Koreans.*

Cycling

Some people cycle around in Korea, although it is a fairly rare sight to see a foreigner on a bike. With a dearth of cycle lanes and the general haphazard nature of Korean roads, it is a somewhat brave choice to take up cycling in Korea unless sticking purely to areas such as parks designed for encouraging exercise. Drivers should always be *very* wary of cyclists in Korea. They are prone to suddenly veering sharply without looking or coming off pavements onto roads. Some choose to cycle into the oncoming traffic

---

* For the reasons given above, I have declined to write what the Korean word for 'crazy' is. If you want to know, you can easily look it up in an English to Korean dictionary!

rather than with it, especially old people. This practice is particularly dangerous at night when many cycle without lights and often wear dark clothes with no illumination whatsoever. It sometimes feels like Korean cyclists have no perception of danger.

D

DMZ

The DMZ is the Korean Demilitarized Zone that was drawn up to divide the North and South at the end of the Korean War. Both sides situate a large number of troops on their respective sides of the DMZ. Interested visitors may go on tours of the DMZ.

Dog Meat

One of the most controversial issues in South Korea is the consumption of dog meat. It is true that some Koreans do eat dog meat, often in a soup called Boshintang (보신탕), however this practice is far from universal. Many Korean people never eat it and even amongst those that do, only a tiny number do so on a regular basis. It is most commonly eaten in the summer and some Korean people consider it to be good for their health.

Some foreigners do choose to try dog meat, often out of curiosity. Foreigners in Korea with a few Korean friends may receive a suggestion to go and eat it at some point. It is unlikely to cause offence if the foreigner rejects the invitation.

Dokdo Island

Anyone who lives in Korea for any significant length of time and begins to take an interest in the news or Korean affairs is likely to come across Dokdo (also known as The Liancourt Rocks) as an issue at some point. Known as Takeshima in Japan, it is an island whose sovereignty is strongly disputed by both sides. A small handful of Koreans live there and the island is patrolled by Korean troops. Any fresh claims by Japan to the island stir up intense anger and patriotism in Korea. Korean school students are carefully and thoroughly educated about Dokdo and some even go on school trips to see the island. Foreigners are often slightly bemused but curious about the issue and some even go to visit to see what all the fuss is about.*

Dramas

Korean people love television dramas. They are particularly popular with women. Some channels show several in one day. The stories are often predictable and repetitive and will be difficult for most foreigners to

* One American I know came back from a trip there feeling very disgruntled because not only was it expensive but also the ferry only went around the island a few times rather than letting the visiting group set foot on it. Others have successfully managed to though. Look into this before travelling.

understand. However, with patience and perseverance, some foreigners will find they are a very useful tool for improving their Korean listening skills.

Drinking Culture

Drinking culture is important in Korea. Koreans see it as a good chance to strengthen personal relationships with work colleagues and friends. It is also a chance for people to relax around each other. While not enjoyed by all of course, for many foreigners working with Koreans it can be a good opportunity to reduce the language barriers. Koreans sometimes become braver about attempting to converse in English while drinking and foreigners too can treat it as a chance to try out some Korean. This can only strengthen bonds.

There are a lot of points to note to avoid the risk of causing offence with regards to drinking in Korea. People should not pour their own drinks from bottles or pitchers and should wait for others to offer them a drink. If someone wants a drink quickly, that person should pour a drink for another person and look to get one poured in return. Drinks are normally poured for the most senior people first. When people receive drinks, they should hold their glass up with two hands rather than one, even if the glass is very small. While some foreigners may consider it unhygienic, Koreans often pass their glasses around and drink out of each other's glasses. Sometimes Koreans may pass you their glass, pour you some alcohol, expect you to drink it quickly and then return the glass and pour alcohol for them.

When drinking in a bar in Korea, it is usually compulsory to order a food side dish with the first drinks. Further orders are not required with later drinks. These side dishes include food such as chicken, pork cutlet, fruit, dried fish and various spicier foods. They are sometimes a bit pricy but after that the beer tends to work out slightly cheaper than in the west, especially if drinking Korean brands. On occasions, foreigners drinking only with other foreigners may try not to order a side dish and only order beer but this can sometimes cause problems or tension and such a course of action is best avoided even if arriving at a bar on a full stomach having just eaten dinner. There are some bars around which are renowned for aiming more specifically at foreigners. In these bars it is sometimes acceptable for foreigners not to order side dishes but check first, ideally by asking another foreigner who is familiar with the bar.

After finishing drinking it is normal for one person to pay the whole bill. This person will usually be the oldest or one of the most senior in the group. Sometimes the same person will pay time and time again. If someone has had something special happen one day like getting a promotion, passing an exam or another impressive accomplishment at work then it is common for that person to treat the whole group. Dutch pay is not the norm in Korea especially when out with older people and even though it may seem like a good gesture to offer money towards the bill, it is just as likely to cause offence or at least a momentary piece of awkwardness all round. Amongst younger generation Koreans the concept of Dutch Pay is now becoming more common.

Drinking and Driving

Obviously driving after drinking alcohol is a bad idea in any country. In Korea, it can be particularly risky, even if the driver only drinks a modest amount and is able to drive without being erratic. Korean police sometimes set up on targeted roads around towns and cities at night and block the roads off so that no-one can turn away once they are on the road. They then proceed to stop and breathalyse *every* driver who passes by on the road in question. Drivers who are alcohol-free have nothing to worry about but for those that have been drinking there is nowhere to hide.

When Korean people drive somewhere but then end up drinking alcohol, they may hire a substitute driver or chauffeur service (대리 운전 - dae-ri un-jon), whereby a company offering this service will send a driver to meet the customer by their car and then drive them home for a few thousand won more than a regular taxi would cost.*

* Foreigners with a car and able to speak Korean reasonably could also conceivably use this service.

Driving

To drive a car in Korea foreigners have a few options; The first method is to exchange their home country licence for a Korean licence, which is then exchanged back to the home country licence when the foreigner leaves Korea. Steps needed in order to complete this process include getting the home licence verified at the same country's embassy in Korea and completing a simple physical examination. The second way is to complete the Korean driving test and obtain a licence while in Korea (see Driving Academies – page 38). This Korean licence can then be exchanged for a licence from the foreigner's own country when he or she returns there to live where the two countries have a reciprocal agreement in place. The third possibility is for foreigners to get an international driving permit from their own country before heading to Korea and take this plus their home country driving licence to Korea. However, this driving permit is only valid for a year so foreigners planning to stay for more than one year may wish to pursue options one or two.

Koreans drive on the right side of the road and may turn right at red traffic lights if no pedestrians are trying to cross the road. Some foreigners driving in Korea may find it difficult to adjust to the Korean way of driving and become frustrated at some of the habits of Korean drivers. Drivers should also be extremely careful of people jaywalking and cyclists who may choose to cycle in either direction i.e. with the on-flowing traffic or even into the on-flowing traffic![*]

Driving Academies

While driving in Korea is not always the most pleasant of experiences, driving academies for obtaining a driving licence offer a potentially outstanding opportunity. When registering with a driving academy, the learner driver pays a fee upfront covering the costs of all the lessons, at a cost which works out significantly cheaper than most people pay in countries such as England, America and Australia. The learner driver is required to pass a multiple choice theory test which has a pass mark that is not especially high, a short driving course test based at the driving school, which is a simulation of various road conditions and then finally a short road test, completed on roads which are often practiced on several times before the test day. Many people pass each part on their first attempt

---

[*] Putting it as diplomatically as possible, driving in Korea is 'challenging.' While people are free to make their own decisions, I would personally try to dissuade any foreigner planning to stay in Korea for a year or less from driving here unless the foreigner is based in an extremely remote location. For foreigners planning a longer stay in Korea, it is natural to consider driving but even then, think carefully before taking the plunge, especially if you are based in major cities such as Seoul or Busan, which are served so well by public transport. Also, strongly consider installing cameras/a black box into your vehicle to try and cover yourself in the case of an accident.

and repeatedly failing is rare.[*]

All in all, not only is it cheaper and probably easier but the whole process can be quick and fairly stress free (for foreigners whose schedules allow it, a lesson may be scheduled every or most days and the total number of lessons needed is usually very modest compared to the number of recommended pre-test lessons in many other countries). The drawbacks are that there are no guarantees of there being any good English speakers amongst the instructors at a particular driving school, which means foreigners may, in some cases, need the help of Korean friends to get registered and possibly even accompany them to lessons each time.

After receiving a licence, foreigners can sometimes exchange it for a licence in their own country upon their return depending on where they are from[†] and in the meantime may freely drive on Korean roads subject to obtaining insurance or steer well clear should they prefer!

DVD Rooms

As an alternative to going to the cinema, Korea has a number of buildings with comfortable private rooms where

---

[*] Having said that, there was the famous case of the Korean grandmother Cha Sa-soon who needed an incredible 950 attempts to pass the theory test!!

[†] Check your own country's policy in advance.

people go to watch a DVD. People can go in a group with their friends or just with their partner as a couple. There are always a large selection of movies both Korean and western to choose from.

E

Education, Education, Education

It cannot be understated just how important education is in Korea. Many parents spend a fortune on private education sending their children to numerous academies or employing private tutors in a bid to get their offspring into one of the best universities in the country. Some even pay to send their children for extended trips to other countries during vacations to learn more English in English camps and other places with varying degrees of success.

After school each day, Korean children often go to multiple additional places of study and are often out most or all of the day during the week. This becomes particularly intense during their middle school and high school years.*

* One extreme example comes from when I went out with work colleagues one time. After an evening out we finished off at a bar after eleven o'clock at night and as we all gathered outside putting people into taxis home, many high school students walked past us INTO the building to begin late night academy classes on another floor.

A famous Korean saying for high school students coming up to their university entry exams is, 'Sleep five hours and fail, sleep four hours and pass.' Nevertheless, elements of the Korean education system have attracted favourable attention from some prominent western leaders in recent times with some suggesting that various aspects would be worth incorporating in the west.

Embassies

There are many embassies in Seoul including those of all the countries whose natives are eligible for the visas needed to teach English in South Korea (subject to fulfilling other conditions – see page 253). Canada and Australia also have additional embassies in Busan. These embassies will post relevant information on their websites in case of emergencies. Some will also allow nationals to register with them so that any vital information can be sent out by email. Embassies are unable to help in serious workplace disputes between foreigners and their Korean employers. In that situation, try contacting the Labor Board (see page 170).

English Banking

Banking in Korea has often been very challenging for foreigners over the years with communication issues being at the core of many problems. While some expats still experience problems, the situation has been beginning to change in recent times with improved internet banking services and more English speaking help becoming available. One of the leading protagonists in this area is

Shinhan Bank, most notably through their Seoul Global Center.

Everland

Korea's largest theme park is Everland in Yongin, Gyeonggi-do province. It has a large number of attractions such as Magic Land and American Adventure as well as a water park called Caribbean Bay. It is very popular and usually extremely busy. Queues for popular rides can be lengthy and time-consuming.

Eye Sense

Most Koreans do not like to directly do or say things to friends or colleagues that might risk causing offence so instead they give and receive visual signals, which other people can pick up on by using their 눈치 (noon-chi), literally meaning eye sense. One example would be for the people in a group who do not like drinking soju or beer. Instead of refusing the glasses of beer or soju which are offered to them, they receive them, perhaps take a small sip and leave the glasses as they are, almost full on the table in the hope that the people they are with will realize they do not like soju or do not want to drink beer on that particular day etc. The use of 'eye sense' is a kind of emotional intelligence and it is important for judging the mood and keeping the harmony of the group at a given time. For instance, there may be times when it is okay to leave a social gathering early, while on other occasions it will not be acceptable without causing offence to the other people present. If foreigners living in Korea develop good noon-chi, it will serve them well in their interactions with Koreans.

F

Four Seasons

Korean people often boast of Korea's four seasons to foreigners, noting how distinctive each one is. Korean summers are very hot and humid, winters are very cold with regular snow, beautiful flowers bloom in the spring and in the right places, such as Mount Soraksan, the autumn colours can be very appealing. Talking about seasons is a popular topic for Koreans engaging in English conversations.

Fruit

Fruit is generally expensive in Korea and at times prohibitively so, especially if buying it in smaller quantities or just before Korean New Year or Chuseok. Before buying fruit, it usually pays to shop around. It is normally cheaper from fruit and vegetable markets or street vendors than from supermarkets. Buying five or ten kilogram boxes of fruit will usually work out cheaper than buying small quantities, excluding when it is on special offer.

Boxes of fruit are one of the most common presents to take if you visit a Korean person's house or a sick person in a Korean hospital.

G

Gay

One question that comes up from time to time is asking how life would be for someone who is gay and planning to teach in Korea. It is not a country in which people are generally openly gay. While it is difficult to find any statistics, it is likely that a good number of gay Koreans keep their sexuality a secret from their family. For foreign teachers in Korea who are gay, it may be a good idea to be extremely discrete both inside and outside of the workplace and also not to tell any Koreans they work with as there is a significant chance this would lead to problems and a lack of understanding regardless of whether the students ultimately find out.

Getting Married

Marriages are largely civil processes in Korea. Once all the necessary paperwork has been correctly completed and stamped, couples are officially married without the need for a wedding ceremony although most do have one. Foreigners wishing to marry a Korean or another foreigner in Korea will need to complete some formal procedures and paperwork at their national embassy in Korea before going to a local Korean district office to complete the process and become husband and wife. Contact the relevant embassy for more information.

Golf

Korea has a number of leading professional golfers, especially in the women's game. There are many golf courses although they are predictably expensive. A very popular alternative is Screen Golf, which is a computerized indoor simulation of golf using real clubs and balls to generate the line and distance of the ball on the computer screen. It is a cheaper way to play golf and also a good way for beginners to try and build up their skills. Screen Golf is a booming industry and these indoor clubs are easy to find in most areas. However, foreigners will have to practise for a long time if they want to play golf as well as the deceased North Korean leader Kim Jong Il who reportedly managed to complete the first round of his life in thirty-eight under par including an incredible eleven holes in one!

H

Hanbok

Traditional Korean dress is called Hanbok (한복). It is big, colourful, expensive and beautiful. It was worn more frequently in the past than it is today. In twenty-first century Korea it is most commonly worn at Korean New Year. It is sometimes worn at weddings, special birthdays (such as a child's first birthday or a Korean's sixtieth birthday) and it is usually worn by performers at traditional Korean music events. Older Koreans sometimes wear it at other times of the year too even when there is not a special event taking place.

Hangover Soup

One of the most renowned methods of attempting to cure a hangover in Korea is through eating a 'hangover soup,' called Hae-jang-guk (해장국). It comes in various forms and many restaurants which sell it are open twenty-four hours a day giving Koreans plenty of chance to attempt to alleviate or prevent a hangover, whether it be on the way home from the bar, on the way to work the next morning or any other time.* This soup is not just for hangovers though and restaurants which sell it in good locations usually seem to be busy, with its twenty-four hour availability also being attractive.

Hangul

Also spelt Hangeul, Hangul is the South Korean name for the Korean alphabet.† It consists of fourteen regular consonants and ten vowels as well as a number of double consonants and digraphs. Many people learn Hangul in a pretty short time and with a bit of effort start to read words quite quickly. While the basics can be reasonably straightforward to master, the language as a whole is much more challenging. For many, it is a very difficult language to learn, especially for people whose first language is English. Nevertheless some of the foreigners

---

* For instance, during my early days in Korea, I was asked on quite a few occasions to join a frequently hungover Korean co-worker for hangover soup for lunch.

† North Korea uses the same language but under a different name.

who make a good effort do make decent progress with Korean during their stay in the country.

'Hello!' 'Hi!'

It is very common for young Korean children to say 'Hello!' or 'Hi!' in big voices to foreigners when they see them around. They are sometimes very cute. On occasions, it can leave foreigners in Korea feeling like a bit of a celebrity!

Holding Hands

It is very common to see young Koreans holding hands with friends of the same sex when they are walking around in public. While female friends do it more, some males do it too. Occasionally Korean people also try to hold hands with their foreign friends while out and about in the streets. Some westerners may potentially find this strange or unsettling at first but to other Korean strangers in the street it is unlikely to draw any special attention and is certainly not going to have any sexual connotations.

Homesickness

Homesickness and culture shock are very real possibilities when moving to Korea, especially for those who have not lived in different countries before. Some foreigners do not take to Korean food, have problems making friends or communicating with those around them. Those living in very rural locations are potentially more vulnerable. Everyone is different and some take the move to

Korea in their stride.

To guard against homesickness, taking a few of your favourite belongings may help and a positive attitude and open mind are beneficial. Try to find out early on where some of the local foreigners gather and how to get there.* Take up as many invitations as possible to go out with Korean people unless you feel there is a good reason not to. Efforts to learn at least some basic Korean (and perhaps also joining a local Korean class) should help the transition into Korean society too.

I

Immigration Offices

Foreigners residing in South Korea must register with their nearest immigration office within ninety days of arriving in order to get their alien registration card. In reality most will do this within a week or two of arriving. This card should then be carried around at all times. Immigration officers have the right to stop a foreigner and ask to see their card although this does not happen often in

* If you are going to Korea to teach and are able to contact or meet the foreigner you replace, this would be useful information to ask for.

reality.[*] Failure to produce the card could result in a fine. Lost cards can be replaced at the immigration office for a small fee. Changes of address while living in Korea should be reported to the immigration office within fourteen days.

While some foreigners do go their local immigration office alone, most will find it much easier to go with a Korean colleague or boss to ensure there are no communication issues and that the right forms are chosen and filled in correctly. Good employers will willingly do this and those with lots of experience of employing foreign teachers are likely to ensure immigration formalities are taken care of right at the beginning of the contract so that the foreigner can get their registration card straightaway.

International Schools (1)

Korea has an ever-growing number of international schools where foreign children from many countries get a western style education, which is in English and usually based on American or British primary and secondary school curriculums. Sometimes some Korean children who have spent time abroad may also attend the international schools. There are also other schools that teach in other languages such as the French and German international schools in Seoul. These schools aim to provide a strong education that will prepare students for western universities.

---

[*] It has happened just once to me in more than seven years and I do not personally know anyone else who has been stopped even one time.

Most international schools in Korea are very expensive. They are usually well beyond the means of teachers of English as a Foreign Language in Korea. Parents who send their children to these schools often have very well-paid jobs in major companies. Sometimes the companies pay the tuition fees for their workers' children.

The top international schools in Korea are able to employ teachers with very strong teaching credentials including at least qualified teacher status in their own country and sometimes a Masters Degree too in addition to plenty of teaching experience in their own country. (See Appendix Three on page 262 for a selection of international schools in Korea).

J

Jehovah's Witnesses

Korea has a fair number of Jehovah's Witnesses. They are usually immaculately dressed in suits and occasionally approach and start conversations with foreigners who are on their own in public places such as bus terminals. They sometimes speak English very well. Beyond 'Hello' or 'Where are you from?', unprompted starting of conversations with a complete stranger is not very common in South Korea as Korean people usually need an introduction through a third party before they engage in meaningful dialogue with someone they do not know so if someone does do this, they will sometimes, but not always, have some kind of religious intention.

Jeju Island

The biggest island in South Korea is Jeju Island. It is located off the south coast of Korea and may be reached by plane or ferry. It attracts large numbers of visitors each year and it is also a very popular honeymoon destination amongst Koreans. When visiting, hiring a car or bicycle is recommended to get around and see the best of what the island has to offer. Mount Hallasan, the highest mountain in South Korea, is one of the most highly regarded attractions there. Jeju Island experiences periods of substantial rainfall in the months of June, July, August and September but remains a popular destination.

K

Kimchi

Kimchi (김치) is Korea's most well-known food. It is made from fermented vegetables with cabbage being the most common. There are numerous varieties sorted by both region and season. Kimchi is usually very spicy and is considered to be very healthy. It is served as a side dish with almost every Korean meal. Kimchi is usually made by families twice a year in large quantities and most Korean households have two refrigerators, one of which is used just for Kimchi!

Konbae!

The Korean word for cheers is Konbae! (건배) Koreans often use this word and like to make toasts when out in big groups. Even if foreigners are only out drinking with a very small group of Koreans it is likely to make a good impression by using the word Konbae and tapping glasses. Try to make an even better impression by bearing in mind that it is respectful for the younger person to hold his or her glass slightly lower than the older person when tapping glasses.

Konglish

A lot of English words are now also used in the Korean language. Computer, internet, Christmas, game and news are just five examples from a huge collection of words. There is also a variation on this known as Konglish. This sees English words adapted or abbreviated into ways in which they are not normally used by native English speakers. Examples include mobile phone becoming 'handphone' (핸드폰), cheating (as in a test) becoming 'conning' (컨닝) and apartment becoming 'apartu' (아파트). Getting used to Konglish may take some time and it is important to bear the phenomenon in mind when teaching too as many young learners will mistakenly use some of these words believing that they are actually the correct English words as used by natives.

Korean Age

The concept of Korean age is one which sometimes

causes foreigners to scratch their heads for months or even years after arriving in Korea. If you ask Korean people their age, they will usually give their 'Korean age'. Korean age is calculated as follows: A person is considered to be one year old the moment they are born. Korean age then increases by one year every year on January 1st. Age does not increase on the anniversary of their birth i.e. their western style birthday.

Some of the quirks of Korean age include Koreans proudly telling you an older age for their age than their western age, whereas most westerners would prefer to be younger than they actually are! Another strange case is that of a child who is born late in a year, particularly the child born on December 31st. Officially, he or she would be one year old on December 31st and then two years old the following day on January 1st making the child two years old before becoming even one day old by western counting! Having said this though, most Koreans will tell you a baby's age in months rather than years in much the same way a western person would.

Korean age can also leave Koreans confused when they ask foreigners their age and get an answer most commonly in western style age. Some foreigners that are used to how Korean age works may actually tell Koreans both their Korean age and western age in response to being asked or the year they were born in to let them work it out for themselves.

KTX

The KTX is an affordable high speed train service most commonly used for travelling between Seoul and Busan, South Korea's two biggest cities. There are also routes to other Korean cities and the network has been gradually growing. Many people find it an appealing way of travelling.

L

Lose Face

It is very important to avoid embarrassing Korean people or making them 'lose face.' Criticizing a Korean person, especially in front of their colleague(s), or saying something negative about an important aspect of Korean life or culture is something to avoid, even if it means avoiding a subject. Some may even go as far as to say it is better to tell a white lie to maintain the peace.

Whereas some westerners would be able to brush such situations off, it can leave a lasting mark on Koreans and damage relationships, sometimes permanently. The concept of social harmony is critical to Koreans in their everyday lives and it is always important to bear in mind the importance for them to save face or avoid losing face both in their interaction with foreigners and their compatriots.

M

Mail-Order Brides

When some South Korean men start to get old and/or if they are poor they often look to countries such as the Philippines or Vietnam for a 'mail-order bride.' There are a number of international marriage brokers in Korea and thousands go down this path each year.

Makgeolli

One of Korea's more popular alcoholic drinks is a rice wine drink called makgeolli (막걸리). It is commonly served cold in a small kettle or pot and is then poured into bowls for people to drink from. It may be drank anywhere although it tends to be consumed slightly more in rural areas. It is often ordered when eating Korean pancakes called pajeon (파전).

Miguk Saram!

As foreigners walk around outside in Korea, the shout of, 'Miguk saram!' is a fairly frequent one amongst young Korean children with another common but slightly less used call being, 'Wehguk saram!'

'Wehguk saram' simply means foreign person or foreigner while the more popular 'Miguk saram' means American or American person. This introduces one small part of Korean culture whereby most Korean children assume that any western looking person is American regardless of the fact they may be British, Irish, Canadian, Australian, Kiwi, South African or even a non-English speaking European.

As time goes by, the number of foreigners in Korea continues to increase and most Korean children now have some sort of exposure to foreign English teachers at their schools and academies. This familiarization with foreigners means many Koreans are no longer surprised to see westerners, especially in cities. Consequently, the calls of 'Miguk saram' are gradually decreasing as are the number of stares a foreigner may get from Korean children or even old people for that matter.

Military Service

South Korea has compulsory military service for all males. It currently lasts for close to two years. There are very few exceptions except for the physically disabled and those with mental problems. Having sons go off to military service is a very sad and stressful time for Korean parents, especially during any periods of increased tensions with North Korea.*

---

* Korean Americans who have American citizenship and wish to go to South Korea to teach should thoroughly investigate whether they are definitely exempt from military service. There have been reports of such people who did not even have Korean nationality being drafted into the army. There is a lot of conflicting information as to what the official policy and military situation is for Korean Americans.

Monday

Many Korean shops, restaurants, places of leisure and other attractions are open seven days a week throughout the year, sometimes closing for a couple of days during the major New Year and Chuseok holidays. Smaller businesses, shops and restaurants sometimes close on Sundays. However, most bigger places will open on Sunday. Museums, zoos and other attractions that tend to attract a large number of visitors are more likely to be closed on Mondays than Sundays, if at all. People planning a trip on a Monday should be sure to double check in advance that their intended destination is open for business.

Mosquitoes

There are lots of mosquitoes in the Korean summer. Sprays are often used for dealing with them while some Koreans buy nets to put around their sleeping area to stop mosquitoes getting in and to ensure a good night's sleep.

Motels

Many foreigners living in Korea go on trips at weekends or during their vacations and require overnight accommodation. A fairly cheap option is to stay in a motel. Guests may check-in from the afternoon onwards and check-out the following morning. Rooms are suitable for one or two people and usually consist of a bed, television and shower facilities. They do not offer breakfast in the morning. They vary in quality and comfort but will usually prove adequate for a one night stay. They are sometimes referred to as 'Love Motels' as they are sometimes used by unmarried couples or even by people having illicit relations!

Movies

Korean movies will be extremely difficult to follow for foreigners except those who reach a high level of Korean proficiency. Some western movies with Korean subtitles are usually shown at movie theatres. Sometimes major blockbuster western movies are released in Korea at similar times or only just slightly behind the western dates. On the other hand several western movies are not shown in Korea cinemas until several weeks or even months after the western release date. Nevertheless, foreigners wanting to watch western movies in Korean movie theatres will have chances to do so. Popular movie genres amongst Korean people include horror, violent action and romantic comedy.

Mr Kim

By far, the most popular family name in Korea is Kim. A very significant percentage of the population shares this name. In most classes at schools about a quarter or fifth of the students have this name. Each class also has several students called Lee. Park is another common name.*

---

* Some Koreans use alternative spellings for these names including Gim instead of Kim, Yi and Rhee instead of Lee and Pak or Bak instead of Park.

N

Name Calling

A big part of Korean culture is that Koreans never call an older person directly by their name. Instead they must use the appropriate title. Within families, they use Korean words meaning older sister, older brother etc. Amongst colleagues they use Korean words relevant to the person's job title or position. If they are with a current or former student from the same university they would use the Korean word for senior. If they are calling people they know in other situations such as sports colleagues they again use the words for older brother or sister. If they do call the person's name, they must follow it with the Korean word for older brother or sister. For example if a nine year old Korean boy calls a twelve year old Korean girl called Minji, he would either just say, 'Nu-na' (누나 – The Korean word used by males when addressing an older sister or other female acquaintance) or 'Minji nu-na' but never just 'Minji'. Knowing how to address a particular person can be incredibly difficult for foreigners attempting to speak Korean but it gets easier with time and practice.

When foreigners speak English to Korean colleagues in Korea, it is normal to call them Mr Kim, Mrs Lee, Miss Park etc. A few may tell you to just call them by their name, especially if they have spent significant time in western countries but for many they will not be used to being called by their name by a younger person and are likely to prefer it if you do not. Even if the foreigner is older than the Korean they are speaking to, it is still common to call them Mr, Mrs or Miss.

If both people are the same age, they may call each other by their actual name although some may stick to titles, especially in the workplace.

Name Order

When writing or saying names in Korean, the family name comes first followed by the given name. As a result of this, many Korean students become confused about giving their name in English. Someone called 김한나 (Kim Hanna) or 이지호 (Lee Jiho) in Korean should, ideally, be calling themselves Hanna Kim or Jiho Lee in English. It seems like a simple concept but especially for young learners getting started in English, it takes some getting used to. Young learners sometimes find it quite funny or strange when they first hear their classmates having their full names called in the English order i.e. given name first and surname last.

Nanta

Nanta is a highly successful Korean musical, which has also been performed in several other countries including America. The story is of three cooks who have to prepare a wedding banquet within the time limit given to them by the manager. Drums and gongs are used frequently through the story. Audience participation is also a prominent part of this show and the action on the stage generates a lot of laughter amongst those watching it.

Networking

'It's not what you know, it's who you know' is one of the most well-known sayings around and it certainly applies more in South Korea than most other places. A lot of the better jobs in Korea are never advertised and are filled by recommendations alone. Taking opportunities to get to know a lot of Korean people and perhaps socialize with them may pay off. They might just know and introduce you to someone who will be able to help in the future. Having business cards to exchange is often handy. Getting to know lots of fellow-expats can also be useful, especially for teachers who aspire to work in universities one day. Some native English teachers in Korea have also found it beneficial to join KOTESOL – Korean TESOL (Membership fee required).

New Year

Other than Chuseok, the other major Korean holiday is 설날 (Seol-lal). This celebrates the start of the New Year by the lunar calendar and always falls in January or February. It is a three day holiday which, like Chuseok, starts and ends with very heavy traffic as family members visit each other.

Many Koreans wear Hanbok (see page 45) during this holiday. A popular custom is for children to do a formal bow to parents or grandparents and receive some New Year money in return (Known as Seh-bae-don - 세뱃돈). A popular food at this time is rice cake soup (tteok-guk – 떡국) and many families play yutnori together (윷놀이 – see page 92)

Nightclubs

Nightclubs are popular in Korea. Upon entry, groups of friends are often required to pay a table fee, which can sometimes be expensive but includes a few drinks and somewhere to sit for the night while not dancing. Obviously lots of young people and university students go to Korean nightclubs but there are also often more older people than normally found in a western nightclub.

Korean nightclubs sometimes have something called 'booking'. This involves waiters trying to play the matchmaker role and introducing women (sometimes against their will) to a male guest. On occasions, roles might be reversed with a man being introduced to a woman. If they do not hit it off, they can quickly go their separate ways.

North Korea

When people make their mind up to go and teach in South Korea, common questions from family members may include, 'Isn't it dangerous there?' or 'What about North Korea?'

At the end of the Korean War there was an armistice to stop fighting but South Korea never signed a peace treaty meaning the two countries are still technically at war. Both countries have large armies but war has never broken out again since 1953 and many Koreans would like the two sides to reunify despite the complications and expense that would bring.

There have been periods of serious tensions. March 2010 saw the sinking of the Korean ship Cheonan, which the south accused the north of being responsible for (a claim denied by the north). This was followed in November 2010 by North Korea shelling the South Korean island of Yeonpyeongdo, killing four people and causing significant other damage.*

There have been plenty of other incidents over the years too while North Korea's nuclear aspirations remain a major cause of concern to the whole region, not just South Korea.

North Korean acts of provocation are often linked to a need to show their strength and to consolidate the regime

---

* I was in Korea during both of those incidents and I was surprised at the relative calmness of both South Koreans and foreigners who had been residing there for a long time. Yes, there was extreme anger and grief but there seemed to be very little thought of it escalating into something much worse. It was more a case of having seen it all before.

in the north rather than a desire to cause an escalation into war. After periods of tension, strong words or threats of a major response from the south often with support from America usually calms everything down again for several months or longer.

Nobody can be sure what the future will hold for the relationship between the north and the south but they have coexisted for well over fifty years without war and hopefully that will continue to be the case. Some feel that reunification is inevitable one day although no one is sure how that may actually come about. Foreigners that are concerned about North Korea must make their own informed decisions about whether going to South Korea is right for them. The number of foreigners in South Korea is continuing to increase but what is right for one person is not necessarily right for the next person.

O

Olympics

Seoul successfully hosted the Summer Olympics in 1988. After two consecutive unsuccessful bids, Pyeongchang made it third time lucky winning the vote giving it the right to host the 2018 Winter Olympics. This continues South Korea's commitment towards hosting major sporting events. Past and upcoming events include the Football/Soccer World Cup (hosted jointly with Japan in 2002), Asian Games (2002), Formula One racing (from 2010), World Athletics Championship (2011), World Rowing Championship (2013) and Asian Games (2014).

P

PC Rooms

Foreign visitors or workers in South Korea without their own computer are able to go to PC rooms or internet cafes. The signs outside will usually read 'PC 방' ('PC bang'). They are very widespread and can be found on most streets. They are very affordable and normally only cost around 1000~1500 won per hour. Snacks and noodles can usually be purchased and many rooms are open twenty-four hours a day. Many Koreans go there too, especially young people who sometimes spend several hours at once playing computer games.

Pepero Day

November 11th is Pepero Day in South Korea. It resembles Valentine's Day with many people buying Pepero for their partners or friends. Pepero are long thin sticks of biscuit and chocolate, which are usually sold in various varieties, coming in rectangular shaped boxes or in smaller quantities in paper packaging. They are sold all year round but their popularity surges in November, especially in preparation for Pepero day itself.

As a teacher, you are likely to receive a fair amount of Pepero from your students as some students come to school with significant quantities to give to all of their friends, although some Korean teachers within schools do now ban their students from bringing Pepero to school. As a teacher, you do not need to buy any Pepero for your students but it makes a nice little present if you have a boyfriend or girlfriend in Korea. They are often sold gift-wrapped in preparation for Pepero Day.

Pets

Pets are relatively uncommon in Korea compared to the west. Having said that, an increasing number of Koreans seem to be keeping dogs as pets these days. Hamsters are also popular with Korean children. Many Korean people do not like cats.

Foreigners wishing to take pets to Korea will need a certificate from a vet shortly before flying. Some animals also need a period of quarantine upon arrival, with the country they are coming from being a factor. It is important to research more up-to-date information before making plans. For foreigners wishing to teach in Korea, note that some employers may oppose a pet being brought along too.

Pet coffee shops are an interesting phenomenon in South Korea, especially the dog cafes where owners and animal go in tow. It should be possible to spot at least one or two in any reasonable sized city.

Photos (1)

When Koreans have their photos taken it is relatively rare for them to break into a big smile, especially if the photo is in a formal situation. Serious and neutral expressions are more common. On the other hand, Korean children love to give big grins with accompanying v-signs! The Korean equivalent to 'Cheese!' is 'Kimchi!' when the photographer wants to see big smiles.

Public Affection

Traditionally a very conservative nation, South Korea is not a country renowned for shows of public affection between husband and wife or boyfriend and girlfriend. While it is more visible than before amongst the younger generation, seeing anything beyond holding hands is the exception rather than the norm. On occasions, old people tell young couples off or clearly express their disapproval if they see them outside and believe they are displaying inappropriate behaviour or intimacy.

Public Baths and Saunas

One source of intrigue amongst foreigners heading for Korea are the public baths (목욕탕 – mok-yok-tang) and the steam rooms (찜질방). Both are popular places for families to visit.* The public baths are segregated into male and female only areas as people bathe completely naked in

---

* Some Korean men even speak of wanting a son so that they can go to the public baths together!

front of other bathers. Some foreigners avoid them like the plague but others try them out at least once and many speak positively of the experience. The steam rooms are also very popular. Everyone is given the same clothes to change into when entering. Males and females are not kept apart in the same way as the public baths. The steam rooms are even a popular place to sleep for a night.

Public Transport

Probably one of the best things about South Korea is its public transport system. The whole country is well served seven days a week and in all but the remotest locations, the transport is quick, cheap, regular and efficient. Taxis are usually roaming the streets 24/7 and can normally be flagged down by arm in the street with virtually no waiting time. There are many buses for getting around town and there is also a train network, which is complemented by very high speed KTX trains between major cities. Seoul and Busan also have extensive subway networks. Public transport tickets in Korea are usually bought one-way rather than as returns for journeys on land. There are also plenty of ferries and planes for getting to Korea's most popular island, Jeju-do.

Foreigners can usually successfully navigate public transport although many might experience the odd mishap during their early days in Korea. Learning to read Korean to at least a basic level will be helpful for using the bus for local journeys where less English guidance might be available. It is also not uncommon for foreigners who cannot speak Korean or are in the early stages of learning to have their boss or a Korean friend write a message explaining where they live ready to show taxi drivers where to go when getting into a taxi. Similarly a location or address can be written in advance when a foreigner needs to go somewhere in particular.

One important point for foreigners to be wary of when traveling to other cities is place names that sound similar. Cheongju (청주), Cheungju (충주) and Jeonju (전주) could all be mistaken for each other as could Gongju (공주) and Gyeongju (경주). There are other examples too. Even when foreigners have reached a level where they can converse at a basic level in Korean, their pronunciation will usually still not be spot on so it is easy for confusion to emerge when buying tickets for public transport even if the ticket vendor has a basic grasp of English. Foreigners should always very carefully check any tickets given to them as soon as they are issued. It is always a good idea to have a pen and piece of scrap paper handy to write down a place name in Korean to reduce any possibility of a mistake.[*]

[*] Some of these similar sounding place names are on opposite sides of the country so be very careful. Even though these sorts of misadventures can actually be interesting experiences for the right sort of person, realistically you probably don't want to end up going to Gongju instead of Gyeongju!

Q

Questions, Questions, Questions (1)

When Korean people meet someone for the first time, it is common for them to ask quite a lot of questions straightaway. Westerners might view the questions as a bit personal coming from someone they have only just met but they are essential for Korean people to quickly weigh up the relationship between the two people. Of these initial questions the most important one is usually, 'How old are you?' because Koreans address people differently depending on whether the other person is older or younger. While some western people do not like to reveal their age, failing to do so in this situation is likely to make the Korean person feel awkward.

Quickly, Quickly!

Koreans do not wait as often as many westerners do. This means that in busy public areas people brush gently against each other fairly often. It is rare for Koreans to apologize in this situation as some would have to do so very often. If a lot of people are waiting at a bus stop in Korea, it is common for a bit of a surge when the bus stops rather than people boarding in an orderly single file line.

Occasionally foreigners complain about Koreans sometimes cutting queues while Korean drivers have often been known to sound their car horn if they do not approve of the slow speed the driver in front is driving at or if the driver is a little late responding to a changing traffic light. All of these points are a reflection of Korean society's 빨리빨리 (bballi-bballi - 'quickly quickly') lifestyle. When Koreans are doing something or going somewhere, they generally like to finish as soon as possible.

R

Rainy Season

Korea has a rainy season each summer known as Jangma (장마). Actual dates vary but it usually starts sometime towards the end of June and lasts for approximately one month. It does not usually rain every day but the rain is frequent and heavy throughout the whole of South Korea during this period.

Red

Do not write the names of people including students and co-workers in red ink while you are in South Korea. It is a big no-no as it is a sign of death and bad luck. Using a red pen for other writing is usually fine. Just be sure to avoid writing names in red.

Red Days

Public holidays are often called 'Red Days' in South Korea. There are more than ten each year, most notably three days in the winter for Seol-Nal (New Year by the lunar calendar) and three days in the autumn for the Korean

Thanksgiving Holiday called Chuseok, which is also determined by the lunar calendar. If a public holiday falls on a non-working day, days in lieu are not given. However, if one of the big three day holidays fall in the middle of the week, some schools may give additional days off, perhaps even making the whole week a holiday. This should not be assumed though and rather be treated as a nice bonus if it ends up happening where you work.

Red Traffic Lights

As a pedestrian, always be extremely careful when crossing the road in Korea, whether it be at a pedestrian crossing or elsewhere. While Korean driving laws permit drivers to turn right at red traffic lights as long as no pedestrians are trying to cross, many Korean drivers take this one step further and sometimes choose to go straight or turn left too at red traffic lights, especially if it is at night, they are delivering fast food, or if the roads do not look busy. Accidents do happen, sometimes with tragic consequences. Always stay vigilant and do not take it for granted that a driver will stop when approaching a red traffic light.

Renting Accommodation

Korea has two ways of renting an apartment or house. One is a system known as 월세 (wol-seh) along western lines of putting down a deposit (which is often a bit higher than one would pay in their own country) and then paying rent monthly. The deposit is returned at the end of the contract. The other method, called 전세 (jon-seh), sees the renter put down a huge deposit which is often close to half the value of the house or apartment and then lives there throughout the duration of the contract without paying monthly rent. Again the money is refunded when the renting period finishes.

When first hearing about the jon-seh/huge deposit system, it may sound like a very high risk way of renting but it is very popular in Korea as it provides a good opportunity for tenants to save money each month. There are also laws to protect the renter, especially if renting through an estate agency. Nevertheless it is not something to enter into lightly. For most foreign English teachers starting off in Korea, debating the merits of the monthly system versus the massive deposit is not something that will be necessary as accommodation is normally provided by the employer.

Respect Your Elders

Korea is traditionally a Confucian society where older people command great respect. This is shown in many ways. When two Koreans bow to each other, the younger person should bow more deeply than the older person. When attending a restaurant in a group, the younger people should wait for the oldest person to sit down first, or if the oldest or highest ranked figure comes later, everyone should stand up on his arrival. Similarly people should wait for the oldest person to start eating first. When drinking alcohol within a Korean group, it is good manners to turn one's head away from a much older person and drink discreetly and as mentioned earlier, seniors should be called by their title and not their name (see page 59). Remembering these rules should stand foreigners in good stead during their time in Korea and help make a favourable impression.

Restaurants

Eating out is such a big part of Korean life. With several restaurants on most streets there is never a shortage of places to go. It sometimes seems surprising that so many restaurants can coexist so close together but somehow they do. Many restaurants have pictures of some or all of their food while others may have the names of each meal in English as well as Korean, especially if they are selling western style food so it is rarely difficult to order food, even if the customer cannot speak or even read Korean. Korean food restaurants usually work out cheaper than those offering a menu providing non-Korean foods.

S

Safety

Foreigners in Korea generally consider it to be a pretty safe place to live with many feeling safer in Korea than in their own country. It is quite rare to hear news reports about knife crime, gun crime or any attacks by Koreans on foreigners. Shops, academies and restaurants are all open until well into the evening so there are usually plenty of people outside long after dark. It is quite common to see children and families out quite late at night as well as many people exercising. However, personal safety should never be taken for granted. There is crime. Women are probably wise to avoid walking alone or using taxis alone late at night and even though there is often CCTV, all people should keep an eye out for people acting strangely near apartments or elevators.

Samgyeopsal

Samgyeopsal (삼겹살) is always a favourite meal with Koreans and also one of the most popular amongst foreigners in Korea. It consists of pork cut into strips and resembles bacon in appearance. Some samgyeopsal restaurants have low tables and diners sit on the floor. Customers usually order their food and quantity and then grill it themselves at their table. It is served with a wide variety of side dishes plus kimchi and people often drink soju with it. Tables commonly have a button for customers to press for assistance when they want to order extra meat, side dishes or alcohol.

See a Doctor

Foreigners can see doctors quite easily in Korea. A quick examination for a relatively minor ailment such as some sort of cold should only cost a few thousand won with a medical insurance card and a little bit more without. Many Korean doctors will know some or many medical words in English but a lot of them with not have the ability to converse particularly well in English so it is usually better to go to a hospital with a Korean speaker if possible. The other problem with seeing a doctor in Korea is knowing which hospital to go to as there are all sorts of different hospitals for a variety of health issues (see Appendix Four on page 263 for additional guidance).

It is quite common in Korea for the doctor to tell a nurse to give patients an injection in the hip if they have heavy colds or are showing other signs of being quite under the weather. After handing in a prescription in the pharmacy (약국 - yak-guk) it is normal to receive two, three or even four different tablets in each packet to be taken thirty minutes after each meal. A three day course of medicine is very common.

Sending Money Home

At some point while living and working in Korea, most people will want to send money to their bank back home. To set this up for the first time, foreigners will have to take their passports, their contract or other proof of how the money was earned and full details of the bank the money is to be sent to. If the Korean bank has multiple branches within the city, it is often better to go to one of the biggest ones as they are more likely to be used to dealing with requests from foreigners. The bank fees for sending money from Korea are usually reasonable although some banks back home might charge more for receiving it, which is something to bear in mind if considering sending money on a monthly basis rather than in less frequent larger amounts.

It is becoming increasingly possible to organize sending money back home online, especially after setting it up with a local bank. This should prove very useful. While some bank workers will speak English enough to make sending money home fairly straightforward, this is sadly not always the case. People living in or near to Seoul may prefer to take advantage of the improved English banking services which are now being offered (see page 41).

Seoul

When people first think of South Korea, they usually think of the capital city Seoul. For some, it might be the only city they know when they start to explore the possibility of living in or visiting South Korea. Host of the 1988 Summer Olympic Games, Seoul is a metropolis with a population of more than ten million people including a significant percentage of South Korea's international population. Seoul is a vibrant city with a well-developed transport network including a comprehensive subway system. Incheon international airport is also very conveniently located nearby.

Many foreigners planning a spell in Korea only want to work in Seoul or at least make it their first choice. Others may prefer smaller cities or somewhere more rural. There are so many interesting areas all around Korea waiting to be discovered that it should not be considered a necessity to live in Seoul. Not only that but also it is fairly easy to reach Seoul from almost any location in the country. Many foreigners live in areas far from the capital and then choose to visit there periodically for a day or even a weekend, taking advantage of cheap public transport and affordable overnight accommodation such as motels.*

Service

When people go to a restaurant or bar or other places offering a service in Korea, they will normally place an order for food or drink. When this is served to the customer by the venue proprietor or worker it will sometimes come with something a bit extra which was not ordered such as an extra side dish or some fruit in a bar or a soft drink in a restaurant. On other occasions, an extra might come later on while you are eating or drinking. When this is given to the customer, the worker will say, 'Service!' That means that they are giving something extra as a free bonus, either because they value your regular custom or if you not a regular, they hope to see you again soon. Obviously this does not place the customer under any obligation but some places will frequently give 'Service' if they do keep going, although naturally this will vary from place to place.

* Note that motel prices sometimes increase significantly at popular times such as Christmas and may fill up more quickly too.

If you do receive 'Service,' be sure to show your genuine appreciation by enthusiastically saying thank you in Korean (감사합니다 - Kam-sa-ham-ni-da).

Side Dishes

Whenever a Korean meal is served it is usually accompanied by a large selection of small side dishes, which will naturally include kimchi. Anyone invited to a Korean household for a meal should thank their host graciously for the food. Even if the cook tries to downplay it, it is likely *she* (in Korea it usually will be the woman of the house who has done the cooking) will have slaved a way for a long time to be the perfect hostess.

Smoking

Some Korean men are very heavy smokers. It used to be a very rare sight to see Korean women of any age smoke in public although it is becoming a slightly more frequent sight these days. Cigarettes are very cheap in Korea compared to countries such as Britain, America and Canada. If you smoke, try to smoke out of the sight of your students if at all possible.

Soju

Soju is Korea's most famous alcoholic drink. It tastes quite similar to vodka and is commonly made from rice or potatoes. It can vary but its alcohol content is usually around 20%. Unlike vodka, it is not very common to mix it with anything and it is usually drunk neat.* Soju is a common sight at dinner outings, especially at meat restaurants. When foreigners dine out with Koreans, they are extremely likely to have soju poured for them.

Soju is served in shot glasses. People should not pour their own drinks. When receiving soju from a Korean, it is good manners to hold the glass with both hands while the drink is poured, despite the smallness of the glass. After receiving a glass of soju, the foreigner should reciprocate and pour one for the Korean person. In some cases, the first person to receive a drink drinks up quickly and then gives the same glass back to the server to drink from. It is normal to briefly turn away from the other person and hold the glass with both hands while actually drinking a glass of soju.

Foreigners who do not wish to drink soju should, where at all possible, avoid outright refusal of a glass and instead either try to insist on only receiving an absolutely tiny amount or take a normal quantity but then put it down on the table and try to avoid drinking it or just take very small sips occasionally in the hope that the other person will pick up on the visual hint.

---

* The exception to this is when Koreans start drinking bombs! This is beer mixed with a shot of soju. This drink is called pok-tan-ju (폭탄주), with pok-tan (폭탄) being the Korean word for bomb.

Soju is particularly popular with Korean men. Some drink it in significant quantities. It is common to see men sat at tables drinking it outside convenience stores with several empty bottles already on the table. Old Korean men often like to drink soju while playing yutnori (see page 92) in parks. The bodies of Korean men often seem to have a very high tolerance of Soju. Whereas western people might ask their friends how many *glasses* or shots of a spirit they can drink, Koreans sometimes ask, 'How many *bottles* of soju can you drink?'!

Song Rooms

Korean karaoke consists of going to song rooms known as no-rae-bang (노래방) and hiring a private room out, usually for an hour or more although thirty minutes is also possible. Couples can go but groups of friends or colleagues are more common. Other customers cannot see you sing although they might hear you as they enter or exit the building. The song rooms are popular places to go at night (many do not open until well into the afternoon or later) and are often used to finish an evening's entertainment off after going out drinking.

After arriving at a song room, avoiding singing a song is not usually an option! If you go to a no-rae-bang your Korean friends will expect you to sing at least one or two songs, whether it be a solo or with other people. No-one seems to hold it against other people if they are tone deaf! There are large song books with pages and pages of English and Korean pop songs both old and new to choose from. Learning even just one Korean song is likely to impress your Korean friends or colleagues greatly.

Spicy

Korean cuisine is generally spicy and in some cases extremely hot. However, for foreigners unable to eat spicy food well, there are plenty of milder alternatives available. Being unable to eat spicy food is less problematic than being a vegetarian in Korea.

It sometimes feels like Koreans think they are the only people capable of eating their very spicy food. If you find you love the hot food there, be prepared for compliments,* periodic surprise or even astonishment from Koreans that you can eat their spicy food so well!

Squat Toilets

Many Asian countries still have some squat toilets down on the ground. Many foreigners are not keen on them. In Korean houses, expect western style toilets. In public places, either is possible and some restrooms often have both allowing people to choose. These days, more and more places have western toilets so someone who is determined to avoid squat toilets should be able to do so the vast majority if not all of the time. A bigger concern might be

---

* For example you might hear, '잘 먹네' (jal mong-neh) which means [He's/She's] eating well.

toilet paper. Be careful not to get caught short. It is always a good idea to carry some tissues around as Korean public toilets do not always maintain good stocks.

Studying in Korean Universities

These days, more foreigners are studying Korean language courses, undergraduate and postgraduate degrees in South Korea. Some English teachers staying in Korea long-term also end up doing Masters Degrees flexibly at weekends while living in Korea. Some courses are offered entirely in English. One big positive for westerners is that it is quite possible to get generous scholarships to study at Korean universities as Korea seeks to boost its number of international students. Perhaps the biggest negative is that there are not many Korean universities which are well-regarded in the west. They are usually conspicuous by their absence in the upper echelons of global university rankings and league tables. Some of the best universities in South Korea include Korea University, Seoul National University and Yonsei University.

T

Taekwondo

Taekwondo began in Korea and is one of the most popular sports there. When foreigners get taken on trips exposing them to Korean culture, a Taekwondo demonstration is sometimes part of the itinerary. Many children attend taekwondo classes at academies. It is a very common sight to see Korean children outside dressed in their taekwondo clothes either on their way to or going home from a class. Taekwondo made its first appearance at the Olympic Games as a demonstration sport during the Seoul Olympics in 1988 and it has been a fully-fledged medal bearing Olympic sport since the 2000 Olympics held in Sydney. Given its origin, it should not come as a big surprise that South Korea has performed very well in the sport since its incorporation into the Olympics, winning more gold medals than any other nation.

Temples

Along with Christianity, Buddhism is a major religion in Korea. There are a large number of Buddhist temples, which are always popular places to visit even for foreigners who do not believe in Buddha. They are beautifully constructed. There are many impressive temples around the country with Beopjusa in Chungcheongbuk-do and Bulguksa in historical Gyeongju being two particularly noteworthy examples. Overnight temple stay trips are also possible with some foreigners praising the experience.

Tipping

It is not customary to tip in South Korea whether it be in restaurants, hotels or anywhere else.* The nearest

---

* One of my generous friends, who was eating in a restaurant while visiting Seoul, once tried to give a five thousand won tip on top of the

equivalent to giving tips is a ten percent service charge sometimes added to the final bill in restaurants. This happens more in establishments that are selling western cuisine but even then there are still many places that do not have this charge. While such a charge is sometimes clearly stated on the menu, occasionally it is hidden well away in the small print and easy to miss, which can lead to a surprise when receiving or going to pay the bill.

Toilet Paper as a Present!

Korean people tend to move apartments quite frequently which means that if you make a few Korean friends, there is a definite possibility of being invited round to their house sometime after they move, whether it be privately on your own or as part of a group of friends or colleagues invited to a housewarming party. It is normal to take a present in such a situation but the most common gift is very different to what you would buy in your own country. The most common presents are probably toilet paper and kitchen roll! Why is this? It is part of a theme of cleanliness so other related presents include other cleansing products too.

While it is not unacceptable to buy a present more

---

bill and the worker seemed somewhat bewildered as if he was thinking either, 'Why is he giving me more money?' or 'Has he made a mistake counting his money?' Quite simply, Korean workers in the service industry are not used to being given tips and do not expect them either.

along the lines of what you might buy in your own country, as with trying to give a tip in a restaurant, there might be a grateful but perhaps slightly puzzled response by the Korean host.

Twenty-Four Hour Lifestyle

Korean life rarely grinds to a halt. Somewhere is always open. Most shops open well into the evening. Bars and song rooms usually stay open until deep into the early hours. PC rooms, billiard rooms and some restaurants stay open all day every day. On rare occasions, some Koreans go out after work, stay out all night and go to work the next day without even going home!

Two Hands

When giving or receiving something in Korea, whether it is a present or even something like a book that you have requested to borrow for a few minutes from a colleague, you should always use two hands especially if the item is being given to you by an older person. To receive something with one hand is usually considered disrespectful in Korea.

V

Vegetarians

Koreans love meat! They eat lots of it and have meat restaurants all over the place. Being a vegetarian in Korea is challenging and for many vegetarians, cooking at home is likely to be a safer option most of the time. One popular vegetable dish in Korea that is served in many restaurants is Bibimbap (비빔밥), which is an assortment of vegetables served with a spicy red pepper paste called gochujang (고추장). However, it sometimes has some meat thrown in or an egg on top so foreigners should ask their Korean friends to make sure it is served without. The Korean word for vegetarian is chae-shik-ju-uee-ja (채식주의자)

Vitamins

Koreans take their health very seriously. However, it can become burdensome on a family's finances. Some buy expensive ginseng and other products. Vitamins are also very pricey in Korea. Foreigners who like to take vitamins every day should consider taking a year's supply with them to Korea rather than buying them after arriving. They also make an interesting if somewhat unconventional present for Koreans. Centrum vitamins are well-regarded in Korea.

W

Weddings

Many Korean weddings are white weddings although a minority may still choose a traditional ceremony wearing traditional Korean dress (hanbok). The actual occasion consists of a ceremony and food, which is commonly buffet style. Weddings are often held in wedding convention centres. The food is usually available before, after and even while the wedding is going on so some guests do not even watch the wedding and just eat and go. Sometimes guests only stay for as little as fifteen minutes and there does not seem to be any obligation to arrive at the time on the wedding invitation card. Of the guests who actually watch the wedding, some tend to talk a lot during it, especially those near the back. The groom or a close friend sometimes sings a song and sometimes the groom also ends up doing some push-ups! Ceremonies are generally pretty short.

When guests go to weddings, they do not usually take presents. The custom is for guests to put money in an envelope before arriving and write their own name on it (Do not use a red pen! – see page 71). A family member will usually record how much each guest has paid in a book. Handing in an envelope with money is necessary to get a ticket to the wedding buffet room.*

The amount guests put in an envelope will depend on a few factors including whether the guest is going alone or with family, how close they are to the people getting married and sometimes how much the people getting married paid if they went to an earlier wedding or similar party of the guests themselves (in which case, it would be

---

* This envelope custom is also the same at other parties such as a child's first birthday party, which is usually a big event in Korea.

common to give the same amount back).[*] If someone is unable to attend a work colleague's wedding, it is common to still give an envelope with cash in, either before or after. The amount paid in this situation is likely to be the same as they would pay if attending.

It is quite normal for two or even three weddings to take place at the same time in different rooms of a Korean wedding convention centre. On occasions, guests from different weddings may eat in the same room. Many high quality photos of the bride and groom are usually on display at the wedding venue as a major pre-wedding photo shoot is done a few weeks before they marry. The photography is usually excellent.

Western Food

Foreigners that do not take to Korean food or just fancy a break from it will often want to eat something a bit more western. These days there are fast food restaurants all over Korea. It has many of the big name western pizza, burger and chicken chains and they are constantly increasing in number. Korean people increasingly like to eat at these kinds of places, with younger generation Koreans frequently going. Korea also has some of its own fast food restaurants, with Lotteria's burger chain being one of the

---

[*] Foreigners invited to a Korean wedding should ask some of their Korean friends what the current going rate is and to recommend how much they should put in their envelope.

most successful.

Foreigners living in extremely rural locations may find their options limited but for anyone in any kind of even modestly populated area there should be some western food restaurants reasonably close at hand. Pork cutlet restaurants are often popular. One of the most renowned places in Korea to go to in search of foreign food is Itaewon in Seoul. It goes far beyond pizza and burger chains and is full of restaurants providing cuisine from around the globe.*

White Day

As in the west, Valentine's Day is February 14th in Korea. Unlike the west, Korea, like Japan, has an additional special day on March 14th, called White Day. In Korea, women should buy men chocolate for Valentine's Day. Men then give candy to women on March 14th. Korea also has another day on April 14th called Black Day. This is lower key than White Day and Valentine's Day and sees some single people get together and mark the day by eating black noodles (짜장면 – jja-jang-myon).

In fact, Korea has a special day for the 14th of every month but other than Valentine's Day, White Day and Black

* Old restaurants close and new ones open but on my most recent visit to Itaewon, restaurants I spotted included Indian, Pakistani, Mexican, Austrian, Turkish, Vietnamese, Ethiopian and even a Paraguayan restaurant!

Day, even many Korean people do not know each of these days well and they frequently pass by totally unnoticed. The full list is: Diary Day(January 14th), Valentine's Day (February 14th), White Day (March 14th), Black Day (April 14th), Rose Day (May 14th), Kiss Day (June 14th), Silver Day (July 14th), Green Day (August 14th), Photo Day (September 14th), Wine Day (October 14th), Movie Day (November 14th) and Hug Day (December 14th).

Won

The South Korean currency is the won. It consists of four different coins (ten won, fifty won, one hundred won and five hundred won) and four different notes/bills (one thousand won, five thousand won, ten thousand won and fifty thousand won). Bank cashpoint machines pay out in quantities of ten thousand and fifty thousand won notes. Cheques (수표 – su-pyo) are sometimes used for larger amounts. Consult up-to-date exchange rate information for details of exactly how much the money is currently worth.

X

Xenophobia?

South Korea is occasionally labelled as a xenophobic country. Is this fair? It is probably right to say that there are elements of xenophobia in Korea but before being quick to condemn, ask yourself whether you can truly say that your own country does not have any xenophobic people. Korea has traditionally viewed itself as a one race nation and until relatively recently, had limited exposure to foreigners.

However, there has been a surge in the number of foreigners coming to and living in Korea in recent times. In addition to this, the number of Koreans spending extended periods of time in other countries and cultures is also increasing. Many Korean adults and probably even more so children, now regularly see foreigners and interact with them. This familiarization is breaking down the barriers of distrust, dislike or mystery towards foreigners, especially amongst the younger generations. While there are no guarantees, genuine feelings of being a victim of xenophobia are unlikely to be a common part of a foreigner's life in Korea. There may be rare one-off incidents but in most cases there should not be anything significant to worry about.

Y

Yutnori

Yutnori (윷놀이 – pronounced Yunnori) is a traditional Korean game, which is especially popular at Korean New Year. It is also common to see old men playing it throughout the year outside in parks or near convenience store, with empty soju bottles by their side! The game may be played by two individuals or two teams. The game has four long wooden sticks (called Yut), which are flat at the bottom and round on the top. The yut are thrown and then points are scored depending on which way up each wooden stick lands. After throwing the yut, the person or team which threw them, move black or white counters around a board, with the goal of getting every counter all the way round. The basics of Yutnori are very simple and can be learned very quickly. It is usually a very enjoyable game.

Z

Zither

Korea has a traditional instrument like a zither which is called a Kayagum (가야금). It is a long string instrument usually played by women. Hanbok (see page 45) is worn for formal performances with this instrument.

Part 2A
Teaching in South Korea

An introduction to Hagwons and Public Schools

Hagwons

The most common starting point of a teaching adventure in Korea is a hagwon (학원).[*] Hagwons can be wildly unpredictable and have been the start of an extremely happy period in the life of so many foreign teachers but for a significant minority they have been a period of stress, misery or even the beginning of a nightmare!

Hagwons are academies or private institutions attended by students after their regular school day and also sometimes at weekends. Parents spend a small fortune on hagwon tuition fees in the hope of keeping their children one step ahead of the competition or at least making sure their kids do not fall behind other students. If parents are not satisfied, they are likely to move their child to another academy. If they know many other parents, they might spread the word which makes life as a hagwon owner busy and stressful but rewarding if successful. Hagwons cover all sorts of subjects including English, maths, art, music, taekwondo and even cooking. Adults, occasionally including foreigners, attend some hagwons too. Some hagwons offer more than one subject (thus students may study one subject for one hour and then another for a further hour) while others focus on just one.

---

[*] Some foreigners also incorrectly use the words ‘hogwon’ or even ‘hogwan’.

Hagwons are all over Korea and there are often many in one town or even the same street. Competition is very intense and many go out of business in their early years. They need to maintain and preferably grow their student numbers to stay alive. One ill-judged idea or serious incident of some kind, failure to attract new students, lack of parent satisfaction or even the impact of a very bad teacher could be fatal or severely damaging to a hagwon.

English hagwons are amongst the most cut-throat of all academies. The English education business is very lucrative in Korea and many people open academies in a bid to get a slice of the cake. While it is possible for them to run with only Korean teachers (especially if they are principally aiming at high school students preparing for the university entry exam), the majority of them employ at least one native English teacher as well. The more they have, the better they are likely to be doing financially. A few of the biggest academies employ around ten foreign teachers or more. Many employ between two and four. Parents like to send their children to academies with foreign teachers and if they make telephone enquiries to an English academy, one of the most common questions is how many hours a week their child would study with a native English teacher.

The basic qualifications needed by a foreigner to work in an English hagwon are very modest. All that is usually required is a degree in any discipline, to be from

America, Australia, Canada, Ireland, New Zealand, South Africa or the United Kingdom, and to be in good health. Additional experience or qualifications such as a TESOL (Teaching English to Speakers of Other Languages) certificate may come in handy but are not essential and many teach without. There are hagwon jobs available with start dates all year round.

Many foreigners arrive in Korea to work in an academy with very little idea of what to expect and no real knowledge of teaching and attempt to learn as they go along. As a result, the quality of teaching is sometimes low or variable. Some foreigners may have problems communicating with and making the students understand them or with managing classroom behaviour. Others may take to teaching quickly and do pretty good jobs from the word go but it will still be a learning curve for them. What many foreign teachers may lack in teaching theory or skill, they go a long way to compensating for it with enthusiasm, passion, a desire to improve and genuine excitement of being in and teaching in a new country.

Many parents are fully aware that many foreign academy teachers do not have any teaching credentials and that some will not be great teachers but they continue to send their children to hagwons. They worry that their children will fall behind if their own kids do not study with a foreigner but other children do. Many also continue with the belief or hope that if their children continue to be exposed to foreigners they will eventually become good at English no matter what.

Hagwons are considerably smaller than public schools, which means class sizes are much smaller too. Many classes have ten students or less and below six is not uncommon. Even the biggest classes are unlikely to have more than about fifteen students. This can be much less intimidating for a new teacher than walking into a public school classroom where the classes sometimes exceed thirty students. That does not guarantee it will be easier to teach though. Students go to public schools because they have to. It is the law and rebelling against the system will be futile. However, most go to hagwons because their parents say they have to, even if the children themselves do not want to go. Many students arrive tired or looking to let off steam after a long day at school and on occasions may pose significant challenges to teachers.

Classes may vary dramatically within one hagwon. Some may be full of students who love English, study well and have a passion for learning. Others may have several students who do not care much for English, do not concentrate well, try to make a bit of trouble or attempt to nod off until brought back into line by the teacher. However, the number of good classes in a hagwon should outweigh the number of challenging classes, sometimes easily so. This is especially the case if the hagwon management supports their teachers when dealing with any problematic students. *

Foreigners teach alone in hagwons. Some hagwons may ask for some kind of lesson plans to be submitted and the owner may briefly pop into a classroom once in a while or look through the door window while the foreigner is teaching but on the whole the foreign teacher can get on with teaching safe in the knowledge that his or her every move is not being watched or monitored. This may be reassuring for new teachers who are sure to make some mistakes in their early days of teaching and produce the occasional stinker of a class or perhaps have the odd problem with a student.

Teachers can learn as they go along in hagwons, correct their mistakes and generally improve their teaching skills and class management skills without alerting the management or other Korean teachers to any minor problems or incidents that take place that might potentially set alarm bells ringing with the owners. This contrasts with public schools where native English teachers usually co-teach with a Korean teacher who will soon pick up on issues such as any struggling foreign teachers having problems

---

* In the experiences of myself and other expat friends in Korea, it seems very normal (but not uniform) for most hagwons to have just a couple of difficult classes with the kids in the other classes being great. Class dynamics can also change for the better or worse as existing students leave or new students join.

with or failing totally to control the behavior or attitude of a class, being unable to excite or capture the imagination of the students, producing ineffective or boring learning materials and activities etc.

Many hagwon teachers work from early or mid-afternoon with classes until well into the evening. (It varies from hagwon to hagwon but expect to finish anytime between seven thirty and about ten o'clock, sometimes with different finishing times on different days). Break times between classes are normally very short and hagwon teachers may teach several classes in a row. Some foreigners enjoy these kinds of working hours as they have the freedom to do what they want in the mornings. Some hagwons also have a kindergarten with even the youngest students normally having English classes too. In this kind of hagwon, foreign teachers may work a fairly regular working day, starting at about nine or ten o'clock and finishing perhaps about six or seven o'clock.

Almost all foreign teachers at children's hagwons work Monday to Friday but some may be asked to work at the weekend for extra pay or very occasionally a regular five day week which includes a weekend day. Anyone teaching adults rather than children at a hagwon will be much more likely to work at weekends and also split shifts (see page 222). A few hagwons may also make their foreign teachers do some telephone teaching (see page 231). Hagwons should make health insurance and pension contributions for their workers but often fail to do so (it is not just foreign teachers that have this problem but Korean teachers too). The worst or notorious hagwons may cheat their workers or cause them problems in other ways. It is a good idea to investigate these points before signing a contract, especially when contacting previous teachers (see Blacklists - page 124, Health Insurance – page 161, Pension – page 196 and Questions, Questions, Questions (2) – page 209)

If a foreigner is very unlucky and ends up in a bad or corrupt hagwon despite looking into the hagwon before flying out, there are courses of action to try. Depending on the nature of the problem, other co-workers may be able to help or the Labor Board might be able to get involved (see page 170). If the situation looks irretrievable the foreign can give in his or her notice and leave quickly even if it means taking a hit financially. If the foreigner really likes life in Korea but just ends up at a bad hagwon, he or she can try again with another hagwon a few months later or consider looking into public schools instead.

Hagwon experiences vary enormously but many foreign teachers have thoroughly enjoyed their time working in one. Many foreign hagwon teachers renew their contract at least once and sometimes several times. Some change hagwons after a year, perhaps moving to a new city in the process or just hoping for a better experience the second time around. In some cases, they may come home for an extended period of a couple of months or longer before heading back to Korea for a second hagwon experience. Other native teachers start in hagwons and then move on to public schools after a year or two having built up their confidence for teaching or perhaps in search of more stability or after having had a difficult time in a bad hagwon. Some move in the opposite direction, starting out in public schools but moving to academies after finding public school life was not for them for one of a number of reasons such as co-teacher conflicts.

While there are indisputably some bad and even terrible hagwons to work in, there are far more good or satisfactory ones around. If this was not the case, foreigners would not continue to go to teach in South Korea in such large numbers. By preparing and researching properly, the hagwon experience can be a positive or even life-changing one. Hagwons offer an exciting opportunity for foreigners to throw themselves into teaching and learn on the job. They also reimburse their foreign teachers for their airfare to and from Korea.

Public Schools

As a new foreign teacher in Korea, the most common alternative to starting work in an academy/hagwon is to teach in a public school. Foreign instructors teach in an elementary school, middle school or high school and in some cases more than one school, which may include a combination of schools such as one middle school and one high school (see Multiple Schools – page

182). Sometimes teachers will successfully apply and sign a contract without knowing exactly which kind of school or how many schools they will teach at until they arrive in Korea. The dynamics of working in a public school are significantly different to being employed at an English academy. Amongst foreigners that have experienced both public schools and academies, some express a preference for one and some for the other.

In principle, the qualifications needed to work in public schools are the same as those required for academies. * Certainly, the same visa is needed and therefore the same conditions apply. However, a few recruiters for public schools may state that some previous teaching experience is needed. One reason for that is that class sizes are usually significantly larger in public schools and it can be very daunting for an inexperienced teacher to suddenly start trying to teach large classes in terms of effective teaching methods and classroom and behaviour management. Nevertheless, the majority of recruiters *will* consider all applicants for public schools even if they have no previous teaching experience. Many new teachers do indeed start their Korean teaching journey in public schools.

---

* There is one notable exception. There is a programme called TaLK (Teach and Learn in Korea), which enables students who have completed two years of undergraduate study at university to teach in public schools. They are paid less though and vacancies are for rural areas only. It is intended as a big cultural experience.

Foreigners who accept contracts to work in public schools work on year to year contracts. A chance to renew a contract will often be offered if the school is happy with the teacher although occasionally renewals can be partially dependant on teaching well during one-off classes observed by local educational officials. Most public schools follow strict salary scales, especially when they get a native teacher through one of the government sponsored programmes. Salary is determined by previous experience (if any) with certain qualifications given some credit. At the bottom end, a teacher with no previous experience or relevant teaching qualifications (such as Teaching English to Speakers of Other Languages - TESOL) will be appointed with a starting salary which is usually slightly lower than that received by a similarly unqualified teacher starting off in an English academy.

As teachers accumulate experience, they move up the scale and see their salary increased. More experienced teachers may reach the top of the scale within a few years with little prospect of further increases whereas academies do not use scales and may have the discretion to increase salaries as they please. However, some public schools run after-school programmes which have the potential to boost a foreign teacher's salary considerably (see page 116).

The majority of public school jobs start at the beginning of March or the beginning of September. Teachers who get their public school job through one of the government sponsored programmes will also usually have an induction at the end of February or August. Not only is this vital for giving new teachers early insights into teaching methods and Korea in general but induction also gives foreigners chance to meet other new teachers and network a bit. This is very useful for settling into Korean life. Whereas academies often employ a few foreign teachers, most public schools only have one, reducing the chances of building friendships or at least having other foreigners to talk to.

Other than the main intakes, alternative start dates for public schools are rarer but sometimes possible. Some schools may have failed in a bid to recruit a foreign teacher and still be looking in April or October. However, note that this is sometimes because the school is in a less-favoured or very rural location. Sometimes openings may appear at other times of the year but caution should be exercised before jumping in. There may be a vacancy because a foreigner has left the school mid-contract. In such a case, the reasons for the previous teacher's departure should be investigated carefully.

Potential teachers should note that if they take a public school job outside the two main start dates, they will not have an induction or at least not immediately although additional training or workshops are occasionally provided through the year. It is sometimes better to wait for one of the main intakes than jump into the first public school job that presents itself. Alternatively, it is worth remembering that academies recruit all year round for teachers looking to start in a month other than March or September.

Public school contracts state that the foreign or Guest English Teacher is an assistant teacher, supporting Korean teachers with their English classes and other English duties. This stipulation is necessary as Korean education laws do not permit foreign teachers to teach regular timetabled public school English classes alone, even if they hold a recognized primary or secondary school teaching qualification in their own country. Normal school English classes involving a foreign teacher must be team-taught with a Korean co-teacher (see page 137). These stipulations do not apply to after-school English classes (see page 116) and English Camps (see page 129) in public schools.

The reality of what actually happens in public school English lessons varies enormously and is highly unpredictable. The native English teacher may indeed be used as an assistant teacher, very much in a supporting capacity as the Korean teacher leads the class. In this situation the Korean teacher may ask the foreign teacher to support students while they do activities and perhaps lead or teach one small part of the lesson alone. In worse-case scenarios the foreign teacher may be reduced to someone who occasionally models to the students how they should pronounce certain words and does very little else (this can happen in other countries too). Thankfully this highly unsatisfying occurrence, while far from unheard of, is the exception rather than the norm.

Often the foreign teacher may be deployed as more of an equal, doing somewhere between forty and sixty percent of the teaching and the Korean teacher doing the rest while both teachers monitor and support students while they do individual, partner or group tasks. This can be a very effective and productive model of co-teaching. The other extreme is the foreign teacher doing all or most of the teaching with the Korean teacher providing minimal support and perhaps just walking around making sure the students are behaving and focused.* Some foreigners like this situation but others may find it daunting leading the class with very little support.

There is a tendency for team-taught classes in elementary schools to be divided more equally between Korean teacher and foreign teacher than those at middle and high schools. It is more common for the foreign teacher to end up leading or virtually teaching alone at middle and high schools than at elementary schools. However, a Korean teacher who dominates and gives the Guest English Teacher very little responsibility could appear anywhere. It

---

* Korean teachers are officially responsible for managing the students' behaviour. Some will take this more seriously and be better at it than others.

is quite common to teach with two or more different Korean co-teachers during a year as they are sometimes assigned to just teach one or two grades each. Co-teachers often change from year to year too. This means that foreign teachers may find themselves in a number of different roles according to the preferred teaching styles of the Korean teachers they work with.

Lesson planning responsibilities can also vary enormously. Some Korean teachers may plan the whole of each English class themselves while others may ask the foreign teacher to plan everything and prepare additional lesson materials to supplement the content of the students' textbooks. In some schools the Korean teacher and foreign instructor may take it in turns to plan lessons or they might decide to prepare one or two activities each per lesson. Sometimes the two teachers may find a time each week to sit down and plan the lessons jointly. Foreign teachers looking for more responsibility with regards to lesson planning and the amount of teaching allocated may wish to bring this up with their Korean co-teacher if comfortable doing so. Some Korean teachers will be pleased to lighten their workload, especially in relation to lesson planning, but some will be more receptive than others to such requests. Bear in mind that ultimately it is the Korean teachers who are officially responsible for the class and free to organize them as they please.

Whichever one of the above systems is in use, it is

highly beneficial to discuss each lesson with each other in advance to be clear of the aims of the lesson and the role of each teacher in those aims. It is also a good opportunity to share ideas for the lesson and it can serve to strengthen the working relationship between the two teachers. It is sometimes necessary for the foreign teacher to make the first move to ensure such meetings take place.

Occasionally foreign teachers may find they end up in a school where one or more of their co-teachers do not turn up for English classes. Whether the foreign teacher likes teaching alone and is comfortable or whether he or she dislikes it and cannot control the class alone is not the main point. It is against Korean education law for the foreign teacher to teach regular timetabled classes alone (as opposed to after-school or vacation classes) and if anything bad happened while teaching alone such as a student having an accident, it could make big problems. If this no-show scenario starts happening at a school, foreign teachers should explicitly request to the school that a Korean teacher attends classes. If this is still not forthcoming, then they should raise it with a coordinator from the programme they were recruited through.

When foreigners have a happy and successful year in a public school and decide to renew their contract, they are usually entitled to take the final two weeks of the old contract as leave to take a trip back to their home country.* In the past, it was common for schools to fully refund the cost of the airplane ticket. In recent times, there has been a move towards paying fixed allowances instead of the direct cost of the ticket, which sometimes means the foreign teacher ends up with more than the ticket cost but sometimes less. Those employed on contracts from March to February are likely to benefit more as they will be flying during less expensive times than those employed from September to August and travelling in the summer season. Foreigners who finish but do not renew their public school contract still get an exit allowance which will usually cover all or a significant part of their ticket home. They will also receive severance pay (see page 219).

When foreigners talk about the positives of working at public schools they mention a number of factors. They like the stability and reassurance of being paid on time almost without exception with medical insurance and pension provided, which is not always the case at academies. Many speak of a professional working environment, feeling respected and experiencing job satisfaction. Some talk about earning significant extra money from after-school

* This is worth checking before signing a contract to work in a public school.

classes.* Others like having more vacation time than they would get at an academy.

When they note the negatives, they sometimes mention language barriers as many of their colleagues cannot speak English well (whereas at academies, most co-workers will have reasonable English proficiency), lack of student contact as those at bigger schools may only see each class once a week or less, periods of deskwarming (see page 149) or issues with co-teachers (see page 137). Some also end up in rural locations and/or teaching at multiple schools involving lots of travel, which while not minded by some, is deemed undesirable by others despite the additional financial allowances that this sometimes brings.

* Note that not all foreigners at public schools are afforded with this opportunity.

Part 2B
Teaching in South Korea

A detailed overview of teaching in South Korea

A

Additional Jobs

Sometimes foreigners may be asked to, or want to work an additional part-time job on top of a regular full-time job. On a standard E-2 visa, this is only possible if both workplaces are in agreement. An additional job must be registered at the local immigration office immediately. Many workplaces will be unwilling to give permission to work an extra job. Indeed, some contracts may have a clause strictly prohibiting it. All full-time public schools have this clause as a foreign teacher in a public school is technically classed as a civil servant. Full-time civil servants may not work additional jobs in Korea, regardless of whether they are Korean or foreign.

After-School Programmes

After-school programmes usually work in one of two ways from a foreign teacher's perspective. First, they can be additional classes taught outside regular timetabled classes but during normal working hours by a foreign teacher in the public school he or she works at.* Students usually apply at the start of a semester if they wish (or their parents wish them) to attend such classes. Some schools will pay

* Not all public schools will run after-school English classes but many do. In recent times, the Korean government has keenly encouraged their expansion as a preferred alternative to children attending academies (hagwons).

the teacher by the hour for these classes. Luckier teachers are sometimes paid per student in the class, which can be potentially very lucrative for the teacher. Depending on how many classes are held per week and how many students sign-up, teachers may be able to boost their salary by several hundred thousand won or more per month for each month the classes run. [*] While regular public school timetabled classes are taught with a co-teacher, after-school classes are taught alone. There will normally be far fewer students in a class.

The alternative format for after-school programmes is for a foreign teacher to be employed exclusively to teach these extra classes which fall outside the regular school timetable. Schools using this system will organize far more after-school classes than those who employ a foreigner to team teach regular timetabled classes. This is one way for a foreign teacher to work in a public school without doing any teaching with Korean co-teachers. It is much easier to get a regular public school contract than one just to teach after-school classes. Teachers who are employed just to teach after-school classes will work afternoons during semester time but will often have their teaching hours changed during school vacations to include morning classes too.

---

[*] Many schools run their after-school programmes for about six months per year. While public school English vacation camp classes may sometimes be similar in nature to after-school classes, they fall under contractual duties meaning no extra pay.

After-school teachers do not usually receive much vacation time.

American English

The majority of places in Korea providing English instruction prefer teaching American English to their students.[*] Textbooks are often American in nature. This may come as a shock to some foreign teachers when they first arrive from Australia, New Zealand, England, Ireland etc. Some foreigners may find that there are more differences between American English and British-style English than they had ever realized. Differences come in several areas including pronunciation (e.g. vase), spelling (e.g. color versus colour) and vocabulary (e.g. flashlight versus torch, [ice] lolly versus popsicle etc.).[†]

There are several ways this issue may be addressed as you teach. Your workplace may try to insist that you teach one particular way (with American English being the more likely way). If this is not forthcoming, then you should be free to decide for yourself. You may choose to rigidly follow the approach of your text book, even if it means teaching American English when you are not used to it yourself. You might prefer to stick to what you know best

---

[*] Indeed, one of the first questions my first Korean employer asked me within minutes of meeting me at the city bus terminal was whether I could teach American English.

[†] See Appendices Five and Six (Pages 264 and 265)

and teach according to the use of language where you come from.

The other way would be to take every opportunity to point out differences in American English and British-Style English as and when they arise but make sure the students have reached a basic level at which they will understand what you mean or you will probably just confuse them. If some students try to assert that you have spelled a word incorrectly when you have used the opposite style of English to which they are used to, calmly but firmly explain the differences in spelling, ideally throwing in at least one additional example if possible. The whole subject of American English versus British English is one that teachers should always keep in mind but it is not something that should be stressed over. Ultimately, it is very useful for the students to learn some of the differences between the two. A reasonable knowledge in this area will help them with the important exams they face at the latter end of their school lives and beyond.

Prospective teachers who are not from America, should not let the American English issue discourage them in any way from applying to teach in Korea.* Moreover some places

---

* I have yet to personally hear of a case of foreigners teaching English in Korea running into any serious problems because they could not teach in a fully American way even if they ended up at workplaces with preferences for American English.

may go the other way and actually prefer a more British style of English. Sometimes academy owners or Korean English teachers employed by them have spent periods of time in Britain, Australia or New Zealand and have become more used to British English. Other workplaces may prefer a good balance of foreign teachers from various English native speaking countries to help give the students a wider exposure to English.[*]

Articles

One problem most Koreans have when learning English is correctly using articles (a, an, the). The biggest reason for this is probably the fact that the Korean language does not have articles. Whereas a native English speaker might say, 'I have a book,' a literal translation of the same sentence in Korean would be 'I have book.'[†] All of this means that Koreans frequently omit articles from their English sentences or use them incorrectly (a elephant, a ice cream etc.). It is very difficult for Koreans to use articles correctly. Teachers should patiently teach and remind students how to use them appropriately. Even after Koreans have studied English for years, this is an area they are still

---

[*] This seemed to be the case when I successfully interviewed for a short-term job at a university in Korea. The department had several American teachers and the professor who led my interview thought that exposure to British English would be very good for the students.

[†] In fact, it would actually be 'I book have' – see page 133 for additional information.

prone to making mistakes in.

Artistic

Many Korean children not only like to draw, but are very good at drawing.* Perhaps this is because many Korean children attend art academies outside of school hours a few times a week in addition to art classes at school. Whatever the reason, it is something to bear in mind when teaching them. For example, doing read and draw, listen and draw or write and draw exercises or games will motivate many students. However, be sure to remind the students that they are in English class and not art class so their pictures do not need to be perfect and should be drawn quickly.

Attention Span

Children around the world have very short attention spans and Korean children are no different. To have a good chance of ensuring the students continue to concentrate throughout an English class, teachers will usually need to provide a few different and varied activities during one class, moving onto related tasks every few minutes. To teach kindergarten children for thirty minutes, a teacher might need four or more activities, as could an elementary school class lasting forty minutes. Older children will be

---

* Having taught in both Korea and England, I would definitely assert that the average Korean student has more artistic ability than the average British student of the same age.

able to concentrate for slightly longer periods of time but will still need fresh stimulus during the course of a class. Activities can include songs, textbook study, story books, games, worksheets, mini role-plays, individual tasks, pair work, group and whole class activities plus many more.

At the Airport

After arriving at Incheon airport (or less often Busan) to begin a teaching contract, foreigners go through immigration, which is usually very straightforward as long as a visa is correctly stamped in their passport. After emerging through customs, foreigners can expect to be met by a representative of their recruiter, government programme or academy and whisked off to begin induction or taken to their new workplace or accommodation. If the workplace is quite a long way away, a recruiter might meet the teacher at the airport and get him or her on to a bus to the relevant city with someone from the academy meeting the incoming foreigner at the bus terminal at the other end.

B

Be Quiet!

Inexperienced teachers are sometimes prone to shouting to get the attention of the students and if that does not work, they shout a bit louder! It is a stressful way of teaching which often does not work and can cause teachers to damage their voice if they shout too much.

Experienced teachers tend to shout less and use various signals when they want the students to stop what they are doing and pay attention. Some teachers suddenly start clapping a rhythm loudly and the students then have to listen and follow. The teacher then repeats as necessary until all students are clapping and looking at the teacher. Another example is for the teacher to press or ring a bell. When the students hear the bell they should either freeze or clap their hands five times and say, 'Attention!' Other teachers may suddenly put both hands on their head without saying anything and when students see the teacher, they have to silently do the same, sometimes prodding classmates that have not seen the teacher.

There are numerous other methods for getting the students' attention. New teachers sometimes develop their own methods. The keys are to make the signals and expectations clear and simple with new classes and train them early on, and also to ensure all students follow the signals. Teachers should start as they mean to go on. If a teacher uses one of the signals and only three-quarters of the students stop talking then it needs repeating (more than once if necessary) until all of the students are following. The use of positive reinforcement (see page 202) can be a powerful tool to help ensure this happens.

Birthdays

Everything related to age seems very complicated in Korea (see Korean Age – page 52). Not only is age usually counted differently to the west, but birthdays are also not straightforward either. Several foreigners over the years have planned activities, which involved the students asking and answering, 'When is your birthday?' only to have the lesson thrown into disorder as many children could not answer despite having the English vocabulary and speaking ability to do so. There are a few reasons for this with the most significant reason for this problem being that some Koreans follow the solar calendar while others use the lunar calendar. While a small number of students may know their birthday by both calendars, many will only know it by one while some students may not even know their birthday by any calendar. When asked about their birthday, they may be confused which calendar they should base their answer on.

If planning to teach a lesson on this topic, it would be a good idea to give students homework the lesson before, telling them to check with their parents and find out their birthday by the solar calendar before coming to the next class.

Blacklists

Over the years some foreigners have had bad experiences at language academies and have shared their grievances on the internet in a bid to ensure other foreigners do not go to work at the same private institution they did. Many have added to existing lists of blacklisted employers. Foreigners who receive an offer to work in a particular academy should consider typing the workplace name and hagwon blacklist into a major search engine to check it out. If nothing shows up, that does not guarantee the place will be a good one to work at but it is a promising start.

A number of academies are franchises so it is also possible that the academy name will show up but in a different location to where the offer has been made. While it is certainly true that some companies have good branches and bad branches it could still be a cause for concern if they show up elsewhere, especially if they appear more than once. In that situation it is up to individuals to make their own judgments but always bear in mind that there is no shortage of jobs to teach English in Korea and there is not a big need to take a risk under normal circumstances.

Black Teachers

Until recently, there were not many black English teachers in South Korea. It is a fact that the best candidate available is not always the person chosen for a job. Discrimination does exist and there are not strong enough laws in place to prevent it. Academies in particular, seem to pay close attention to the photos of potential teachers (see page 200) and opt for someone they like the look of, based on their own perceptions of an ideal teacher or preferences for a male or female teacher and the age range they have in mind.

The number of black teachers or others of non-white ethnicity is now increasing. Black teachers usually find it easier to gain employment in public schools than academies and many have very positive experiences teaching in Korea. However, it is a sad indictment that a very small minority of recruiters find it necessary to write a note of caution on their website that while they welcome applications from teachers of non-white ethnicity they sometimes find it difficult to place such teachers in suitable employment.

Bow

Korean people bow a lot. Many Koreans will bow several times per day and in many different situations. They will bow when they first meet someone, with the person who is younger or lower in status usually bowing more deeply than the other person as a mark of respect. They often bow when they meet relatives. They may do a small bow to a person who has helped them with something maybe in a workplace or in a shop, especially if that person is older. Many Koreans even give a small bow before serving to a colleague in tennis or volleyball!

In public schools, teachers frequently bow to each other. A small bow from both teachers will commonly form part of morning greetings and the goodbye at the end of the day regardless of the age and gender of the teachers greeting each other. Teachers often also give a slight bow to other teachers as they pass them in corridors during the school day even when no dialogue takes place. On occasions, students will sometimes bow too as they see teachers around the school* and sometimes the whole class will bow to the teacher both before and after a class. Foreign teachers working in public schools can make a good impression by following this kind of protocol around the school. A lot less bowing takes place in academies but it would still be good to accompany a greeting to your director or manager with a small bow as an act of respect.

Breaking Contracts

Sometimes a foreigner feels the need to leave a teaching job in mid-contract. Reasons include a sudden need to return home as soon as possible, severe homesickness, to move to a different job in Korea or to get away from a bad workplace.

Most Korean public schools and academies are very unhappy if a foreigner suddenly hands in their notice. It can be very difficult for them to find a new teacher at around a month's notice. Unless they already personally know a new teacher who could take over, they will often have to use a recruiter to find a replacement teacher, which is very expensive. Even if a new teacher can be found, that person then needs to organize a visa quickly.

---

* This might come as quite a shock sometimes when or if it happens to you, especially if you have taught in a western school before!

Korean employers are unlikely to be very understanding if a foreigner does decide to leave mid-contract. If there are genuine family reasons (or they are led to believe that there are) such as a sick relative, they may be more sympathetic, especially as family is so important to Koreans. However, even this will not have much an impact in extreme cases.

Most contracts have some sort of clause stating that the foreign teacher will repay their airfare or entry allowance provided by the employer if they leave before completing at least six months of a twelve month contract. Some but not all will also deduct housing deposit payments for the first three months of a contract to be repaid in full at the end provided that all bills are paid and the accommodation is left in good condition. These clauses are there to discourage people breaking contracts.

Many teachers experience problems after giving in their notice in mid-contract even if their relationship had previously been strong with their boss. These problems tend to be significantly greater for those working in academies. Even if the teacher is more than six months in to the contract and therefore unlikely to be liable for refunding the airfare, it is common but not universal for academies to make massive deductions from the final month's salary giving all sorts of reasons to the point that the teacher is left with virtually no pay for the month. Many workplaces will refuse to sign a letter of release if the teacher is not going home but rather looking to move into another job (see page 179). Some academies also try to claim that the foreign teacher may not leave or try to insist he or she stay for another two or three months (and then sometimes another one or two months) or until another teacher is found.

Due to the various problems that can occur after handing in notice at an academy, sometimes foreigners consider it better to do the infamous 'Midnight Run' (see page 180). In the interests of balance, it should be noted that premature partings of ways do not always end in tears and can be relatively civil. However, it needs to be borne in mind by foreign teachers in Korea that real problems with breaking contracts occur frequently enough to make it a distinct possibility.

C

Camps

Summer camps and winter camps are additional English programmes put on by public schools, universities and other places for young learners during school vacations. They are normally a compulsory part of a foreign teacher's public school contract for a few weeks each vacation and usually do not provide any extra pay (only standard monthly salary). Occasionally, very remote rural public schools may not run camps during the vacation, giving lucky foreign teachers extra vacation. University instructors may find themselves teaching children's camps too although these are sometimes optional and often for additional pay.

These vacation camps come in various guises. Teachers may be asked to just teach from books, running classes not too dissimilar to regular semester time classes. Sometimes though, classes will mark a significant shift from normal term time ones. Teachers may be asked to prepare all sorts of activities such as crafts, cooking or plays and other performances to be attempted through the medium of English. Often the emphasis will be concentrated on ensuring students have fun while using some English.

Sometimes education providers need additional teachers on short-term contracts for these camps. Some universities give their foreign teachers permission to work at camps elsewhere. There are also potentially chances for new teachers to fly over and come and sample what working in Korea is all about. These experiences could be invaluable either as standalone contracts or for those teachers that are interested in the possibility of teaching in Korea but do not feel ready or confident enough to commit to a one year contract.

Foreigners who come to Korea just to do a camp initially should note that they still need a visa (C-4 Visa) and their airfare will not always be paid for them or only partially so, which means they will struggle to make any money overall. However, the camps usually pay reasonably well so for the experience they provide, they are an interesting option.

Change

Korean public school teachers usually move schools every four years. They cannot usually stay longer, even if they want to. * In some cases they may even change schools before four years have elapsed. From a foreigner's point of view this may mean instability. Co-teachers may change frequently, even from year to year. This can be frustrating, especially if good working relationships have been built. Conversely it can work the other way. If a foreign teacher likes a school but not one of the co-teachers, by being patient, a more 'desirable' teacher may come along the next year. If you find yourself in this situation, consider casually asking how many years the teacher has left at the school to see if it is worthwhile trying to outlast the teacher you are having problems with.

* This rule does not apply to foreign teachers in Korean public schools. If both parties are happy, foreign teachers may be able to continue for many years in the same school (subject to renewing their visa). There are no restrictions at English language academies either. However, some Korean universities have limits for their foreign teachers such as a maximum of three years or a set number of contract renewals.

Children's Songs

Songs are a great tool for using with young language learners. Textbooks will usually be accompanied by a CD containing songs and chants linked to units of study. These are variable in quality but young children love to sing and learn good songs and they are very useful for practising English expressions and vocabulary. YouTube has so many great clips for showing and using in the classroom. It is an absolutely invaluable resource. There are so many English songs on there to choose from. Four very popular examples are; Alphabet Song (Vol 1) Toonbo.com; The Number Rock; I am a Pizza (With Korean Subtitles); The Skeleton Dance (Updated Version).

Classroom English

One of the biggest mistakes made by teachers, especially those just starting out, is to talk at far too high a level for the students using difficult vocabulary or complex sentences which the students cannot understand. New teachers should consider using the internet to research or find lists of commonly used straightforward phrases, commands, questions and responses for teaching English as a Foreign Language before starting to teach. Some language textbooks also have a page or two of classroom expressions at the beginning of the book for reference.

Class Size

The likely number of students in a class is something that may be an important factor in some people deciding where to work in Korea. Some teachers may prefer small class sizes while others may prefer larger ones. Each has advantages and disadvantages. There will usually be somewhere between about four and fifteen students in most academy classes while many public schools will have regular class sizes of between twenty-five and about thirty-five students.* Additional public school classes such as after-school programmes and vacation classes will sometimes have far fewer students. Public schools in very rural locations will have much smaller class sizes and may even combine students of different ages into one class.

Common Mistakes

There are a number of recurring mistakes that many Koreans make when learning English. It is very useful for teachers to be acquainted with examples so that they can provide students with additional practice and exercises in these areas as and when the need arises. One major example is Koreans mixing up the word order of English sentences, caused in a large part by the fact that English uses a subject-verb-noun sentence construction pattern whereas the Korean language uses a subject-noun-verb formation instead (e.g. I-like-you Vs I-you-like). Others include not using plurals well and thinking that Konglish words (see page 52) are true English words. Time is another

* While this is still a lot of students, public school class sizes of fifty or sixty students were common in Korea just a few decades ago. Falling birth rates have led to these declines.

topic that causes problems. Many students will add o'clock to any time and not just on the hour e.g. 1:15 o'clock, 2:40 o'clock etc. One error commonly made by young learners which always provides amusement is getting chicken and kitchen muddled up!

Consolidation of Learning

Most students have to hear and/or see new vocabulary and sentences several times before they stick in their mind. The student who can grasp something the first time most times is very special indeed and the exception rather than the rule. This means that consolidating previous learning is so important.

Inexperienced teachers are often given a textbook to teach and fly through it very fast enabling students to soon move up to the next book in the series. However, the students have often not truly learned what they have studied because they have not been given the chance to practise what they learned in sufficient depth.

To enable students to piece together what they have studied, regular reviews of learning and additional chances to use the key language points are needed. Each lesson should finish with some kind of short review or mini game or activity which gives students a final chance to use, see or hear the target language in action again. Similarly the start of the next lesson is a good time for a brief recap of what was studied in the previous lesson such as by showing picture cards and asking students to make sentences with the language they used last time.

Corporal Punishment

One of the aspects many foreigners find most troubling about working in South Korea is the long-standing and continued use of corporal punishment by some teachers in academies and particularly in public schools. Although some laws have been enacted to officially limit or ban its use, in reality the practice has not disappeared and does not show any real signs of doing so any time soon. Many parents are not against its controlled use in moderation. Overall, teachers themselves are strongly opposed to any moves to outlaw it.

In public schools, foreign teachers may find themselves teaching with a co-teacher who hits students (sometimes frequently). This may be with some kind of stick (sometimes affectionately known as a 'love stick') or even some kind of slap by hand. In some cases, co-teachers may choose only to hit students in other subjects when they are teaching alone and out of sight of foreign teachers. Other teachers will just do what they normally do, regardless of the presence of a native teacher.

For foreigners opposed to corporal punishment who witness such methods of disciplining students, it can pose a dilemma or otherwise be an uncomfortable sight. Should they confront the teacher in private, should they explain that it makes them feel uncomfortable and suggest the teacher avoids such punishment or should they stay quiet about it?

Taking a strong principled stand against corporal punishment may seem like the right course of action but there is a high chance it will harm the relationship with the Korean teacher in question, perhaps permanently (regardless of whether the Korean teacher does or does not subsequently stop hitting students in English classes), making the remainder of the contract very uncomfortable or unpleasant. The Korean teacher may also get word to other teachers that the foreign teacher is a bad teacher, troublemaker or something else along those lines. Still, for some teachers that might be a price worth paying. It is something people have to decide for themselves.

Despite all the controversy and debate over the issue, it is important to note that not all Korean teachers do hit their students - far from it.[*] Some foreign teachers may never teach with a teacher who uses corporal punishment. Some Korean teachers never hit their students anyway, while others have reduced or stopped doing so in recent years. In recent times, occasional footage of Korean teachers hitting students (sometimes quite severely) has

[*] I taught with several different Korean co-teachers and only one of them regularly hit students. The majority of the other teachers never did so.

been recorded by students on mobile phones and caused big scandals. This has probably contributed to some teachers rethinking their approach to discipline.

While some people fondly endorse the old saying, 'When in Rome, do as the Romans do,' this most certainly does NOT apply to foreign teachers tempted to use a bit of corporal punishment themselves against especially troublesome Korean students. While many Korean teachers continue to use it and get away with it unless they are particularly severe, a foreigner would be highly unlikely to be so lucky. Chances are that if parents found out, the foreigner would be strongly disciplined and possibly sacked or worse. The ensuring scandal would probably see an outpour against other foreigners and negative generalizations and stereo-typing of foreign teachers in Korea as a whole. This is to be avoided at all costs.

If foreigners feel that they need to punish students, or at least deter them, they should use other methods (see page 206). They should also remember prevention is better than cure and use some methods of positive reinforcement in the first place (see page 202).

Co-teachers

It has often been suggested that co-teachers make or break a foreign teacher's public school experience. It is not unusual to hear or read about foreign teachers complaining about their co-teachers. However, others will say how good life is when getting good and helpful ones.

Co-teachers are an essential part of a foreign English teacher's Korean public school life. They are not just teachers that native English teachers work with, they are teachers that foreign instructors *must* teach with i.e. team-teaching. If working in a public school, co-teachers are non-negotiable even if the foreign teacher is extremely well-qualified and experienced. This is due to Korean educational policy.

Depending on the size of the school, a foreign teacher will usually have two or more co-teachers for teaching timetabled classes with. One of these co-teachers will usually also be responsible for the non-teaching aspects of the foreign teacher's job such as sorting out administrative matters, organizing any school English competitions or events, arranging contract renewals, setting up vacation or after-school classes, acting as a go-between if a non-English speaking colleague needs to give information to or receive it from the foreign teacher, relaying other important information and sorting out other issues as and when they arise. Some of these head co-teachers perform their role very well, others less so.

Problems can arise for a number of reasons. Some foreigners may feel that in the classroom they are not being given enough help and left to do everything even when there are some classroom issues while others may complain of not being allowed to do much teaching and feeling unimportant or as if the Korean teacher has no trust, faith or respect in the ability of the native English teacher. A common complaint outside of classes is that important information is either not relayed or when it is, not in a timely manner. More serious grievances include that the Korean co-teacher cannot speak English or not at a level which is good enough for effective communication. Rarer are suggestions that a co-teacher is downright difficult or unpleasant.

Before suggesting solutions, it is useful to understand why some of the above problems occur. Co-teachers who just stand or sit at the back of a classroom and do little or nothing may do so because they have no confidence in their own English ability or because the school has invested a lot of money in a native teacher who can use English far better than they will ever be able to do.* They may just assume this is what the foreign teacher wants i.e. to teach alone. (It may be true that on rarer occasions, they see English class as a good opportunity to have a bit of a rest!)

On the other end of the spectrum, the all-controlling Korean teacher who virtually excludes a foreign teacher from a meaningful role in English classes may do so

---

* Note that being able to use English better certainly does not automatically mean being able to teach English better.

for a number of reasons. They are ultimately responsible for the class in the eyes of the law so they may want to keep everything pretty much under their control. Many will have better qualifications than their foreign co-teacher such as their public school teacher license and often many more years of teaching experience too so it can be hard for them to hand over major responsibility to a foreign teacher, especially if they do not highly rate the teaching skills of the guest teacher or if the foreigner is much younger. (Remember that Korea is still a very hierarchical society.) Others often worry that if they give too many teaching duties to the foreign teacher, the students will get out of control – a fear which is sometimes justified and at other times not. Some Korean teachers may get it into their heads that foreign teachers are unable to have a big role because they cannot speak Korean. On other occasions, Korean teachers may simply not realize how much they dominate or exclude foreign teachers from English classes.

With regards to important information not being relayed by co-teachers, it should be noted that it is not just foreign teachers who have problems with this. Leaving things to the last minute is very common in Korea and Korean workers suffer too. Also remember that teachers are very busy and will have several things to think about at once. Innocently forgetting to tell a foreign teacher something may happen on occasions. It is when it happens all of the time that it becomes a bigger problem.

If a Korean co-teacher is hardly able to communicate in English it can be incredibly frustrating. A foreigner can perhaps be forgiven for thinking, 'How can you teach English when you can't even speak English?' but in this situation it is important to remember why there are so many native English teachers in Korea in the first place. Their presence has been a key part in education policy for raising English standards in Korea to a level where at some point in the future, the need for foreign English teachers recedes.*

There are a number of ways to try and solve problems. Most important is to try and build up a good working relationship. Make teachers comfortable to try and talk to you even when or if their English is not great. Always be polite and reassuring. If they tell you their English is bad, try to make it clear that this is not the case. Give them confidence by praising them or noting that they seem to have improved their English a lot recently or since you first met them. Also be welcoming. If you are allocated your own classroom or office to use outside of lesson time, invest in a kettle. Offer to make teachers tea or coffee if they drop by and do not look rushed off their feet.

* Just to be clear, there are also many co-teachers around who speak English very, very well and will be a joy to communicate with and easy to talk to.

When colleagues do a good deed in Korea it is quite common for the recipient to drop by the other teacher's classroom and give them something small later in the day or the next day as a token of appreciation. A small bottled drink of juice (about 150ml) tends to be the most popular gift for this purpose. If your co-teachers like you, they are more likely to be open to helping more in classes if you ask them to do so. Teachers that tend to dominate may become more willing to consider letting you plan some classes and lead some of your great activity ideas for class or give you a bit more responsibility in class so that you can develop your teaching skills.

Korean co-teachers who agree or nod their head to foreign teacher requests only for nothing to happen, may not actually understand what is being asked of them (see Agreeing – page 22). If the school has an internal email system, it can be worth sending a reminder later after the verbal request as most Koreans can understand written English better than spoken English. If this is not an option, it is important to remember to communicate wishes in simple language. It is very common for foreigners new to Korea to talk to colleagues and even very young students in almost exactly the same way as they would to their friends back in their home country. This is often very ineffective! Avoid very long sentences, difficult vocabulary or slang and slow the talking speed down a bit to improve chances of co-teachers understanding what it being asked of them.

If there is a major communication problem related to something important such as a contract issue or a different serious co-teacher related problem, it may be useful for a foreigner to contact the regional office of whichever government-sponsor programme they were recruited by. For many foreign teachers this is never likely to be necessary.

One more important thing to bear in mind related to any co-teacher problems is the need for some honest self-reflection. Not all problems or clashes between Korean co-teachers and their foreign teachers are the fault of Korean teachers despite what some current or former foreign teachers might want to suggest! There may be blame on both sides (such as neither making any attempt to understand each other's different cultures) or purely on the foreign teacher's part. Foreigners should ensure they stay professional at all times and always show their Korean co-teachers the same level of respect and courtesy they expect in return. They should put forward suggestions in a positive and non-confrontational way (such as desired changes in the way English is being taught together). Avoid doing or saying things that may make the co-teacher lose face, especially in front of other colleagues or students.

If things do not work out with one or more co-teachers and the situation seems irreversible there are a few points to remember. School life and co-teachers can change from one year to the next (see Change – page 131). If a new workplace is desired, contracts are only year to year so foreign teachers are never trapped for too long. Teachers that decide co-teachers are not for them but wish to stay in Korea for longer, could move to an academy (hagwon) where they are sure to teach alone or they can even try to get a job at a university in Korea. Teachers who conclude that public schools have many good points but that they have been unlucky with their current co-teachers may just opt to move to another public school with brand new teachers. They may well be luckier the second time around. There truly are a lot of good co-teachers around too.

This section has outlined some of the pitfalls that *can* occur with co-teachers and suggested some ways to minimize chances of these happening. However, the word 'co-teacher' should not immediately bring a groan or other negative reaction. Many foreign teachers who have really enjoyed their time in public schools have done so largely because of their co-teachers. Many have received outstanding support and built up great relationships, really enjoyed teaching with their co-teacher and have socialized together and sometimes kept in touch after leaving the school.

Couples (Both Teaching English)

Sometimes a husband and wife or boyfriend and girlfriend wish to go to Korea together and teach. Someone single sometimes saves a lot of money in a year so the savings potential for a couple is very good. Additionally, going with a partner has the added advantage of reducing feelings of apprehension, loneliness and homesickness, which many teachers face. Of course, both the male and female would need to cover the criteria needed to get visas for teaching.

Naturally, many teaching couples would prefer to live together and quite possibly work together too. If they are able to arrange this, it may be possible in some cases for one half of the couple to receive an additional housing allowance worth a few hundred thousand won in lieu of accommodation. In reality it does not always work out this well.

Public schools usually only have one foreign teacher so it would be rare to work with a partner or spouse in public schools. Both could work in separate schools at the same time and earn good money but if unlucky, these schools could actually end up being a fair distance apart. This is because if foreigners apply for public school jobs through a government sponsored programme, they usually apply to work in a province, not a particular school. Applicants do not always learn of their exact location until very late on and thus couples could end up working a significant distance away from each other. Couples working in public schools may be allocated a slightly bigger house for them to live together if requested but that should not be taken for granted. They might end up with one small apartment each although there would not usually be anything to stop them spending all their free time together in just one of those apartments.

Individual academies sometimes need more than one new teacher at once so the chances of couples working together at academies are greater than at public schools. Occasionally, academies specifically advertise for couples and will provide a house or apartment for them to live in together. Even if they do not advertise for a couple, they might be prepared to consider it. On the other hand, some academies will be reluctant to hire couples especially if they are unmarried. The academy owner may fear the couple falling out midway through a contract and then either one or both suddenly wanting to leave at short notice. Also many older Korean people are very conservative, so some academies owners may disapprove of unmarried couples wanting to live together. It is still pretty uncommon for a Korean man and woman to cohabit prior to marriage.

All things considered, it is possible for couples to go to Korea and live and work together but they may have to wait a little longer to find the right opportunity than people going alone to teach. Also it is very important to remember that when an opportunity for a couple does present itself, they should not rush in to a decision. They should take all the same precautions as someone wishing to go alone. Potential workplaces need carefully checking out and current, outgoing or former foreign teachers of the school or academy should be contacted whenever possible.

Couples (Both Teaching in International Schools)

Possibly the best route for western couples wishing to teach and live together in South Korea is to work in international schools, teaching a western curriculum. International schools actively recruit teaching couples. In fact, being a teaching couple seems to be an advantage in the recruitment process. Contracts are often for two years in contrast to English teaching in public schools or language academies where almost all periods of engagement are one year. This increased stability is probably a positive for most teaching couples.

Unfortunately the international school pathway will not be an option for many couples as the fully accredited schools only employ those who are qualified to teach in primary or secondary schools in their own countries. However, for those couples that do fulfill the necessary criteria, international schools are worth looking into (see page 165 for more information).

Couples (One Teaching English)

If a couple want to go to Korea but only one of them will teach English, the other may apply for an F3 visa if they are married. It is a dependents visa. They may get this visa for their children too if they have any. People are not allowed to work on an F-3 visa.*

Occasionally one half of a couple may get a job in a different field while the other teaches English. There are a number of I.T. professionals in Korea from the west. Sometimes westerners working in various fields in international companies get transferred to Korea.

If an English native speaker is suitably qualified to teach in Korea and is married to someone from a different country such as Germany or France, the non-English spouse may also be able to get a job in Korea teaching their own native language although vacancies may be in short supply. Of course they would also need a visa. They would also need a degree from their own country. To teach languages other than English in Korea, universities and foreign language high schools would be good places to search for jobs.

D

Dating Co-workers

Sometimes a foreigner in Korea may wish to start up

---

* Think carefully about living in Korea with school age children, especially if sending them to an international school is not an option. They would probably find it tough going in a Korean public school without a good grasp of Korean.

a relationship with a Korean co-worker. In many countries people meet their partner at work but nevertheless workplace romances are often considered as an area to tread carefully and Korea is no exception. If anything, more caution should be exercised than in one's own country. It is unlikely that academy owners or public school principals or vice-principals will be happy if they hear of a relationship between their workers, even less so if they are very conservative. Any subsequent break-up is likely to be problematic for the foreign teacher while remaining in the same workplace.

A safer course of action would be for foreigners to ask their Korean co-workers to introduce friends who are single or to wait until changing workplace or the person they like moves before trying to get together. However, for those that cannot wait, it is obviously perfectly possible for there to be a happy ending but tread very carefully along the way, especially in the early days. Also note that married public school teachers cannot work in the same school in South Korea so if two teachers in the same school get together and subsequently marry, one teacher would have to move to a new school at the end of the school year.

Deskwarming

This is a term used mainly in a negative context by foreign public school teachers in Korea, which describes having to stay in their classrooms when they have several hours, a whole day or even longer without any classes either due to gaps in their schedule or the cancellation of classes. Foreigners who complain about deskwarming believe that they should be allowed to go to work late, go home early or stay at home if they do not have any classes at a certain time for any reason. This overlooks the fact that their Korean colleagues are not afforded such privileges either during regular semester time.

The viewpoint of some foreign teachers perhaps becomes a bit more understandable during school vacations when additional classes or camps are sometimes combined with periods of inactivity which are often accompanied with an obligation to remain at school, while Korean teachers are not bound by such restraints and may stay at home. However, some Korean teachers are often as busy during school vacations as they are during semester time with additional training courses or work towards graduate degrees, which is a fact some foreign teachers are unaware of or disregard.

Some foreigners happily or otherwise waste the deskwarming hours away on the internet. However, the most positive approach to deskwarming is to treat it as an opportunity. Use the extra time to prepare better classes and exciting or stimulating lesson resources to aid the students' learning. Another possibility is to invest the time in personal development such as working towards a master's degree or other qualification, possibly through distance learning. Many foreigners use these periods studying some Korean, which is also a very good way to invest the time.

Prospective teachers who do not like the thought of the possibility of some periods of deskwarming may prefer to work in academies where it is less prevalent but usually counter-balanced with more classes per week.

Do You Understand?

An all so familiar sight in classrooms not only in South Korea but also around the world is for teachers to explain a task to students and then ask, 'Do you understand?' Often students then all answer, 'Yes!' in unison only for nothing to happen and a look of bewildered faces when the teacher gives the go ahead to start the activity or piece of work. This happens even more frequently with student teachers or other inexperienced teachers.

Why does this happen? There are two reasons that particularly stand out. First of all, many students do not like to admit they do not understand or to show other signs of weakness. Secondly, if a task is only explained orally without visual aids, students are less likely to understand.

Whenever possible, demonstrate an activity in a visual way making use of props, classroom board and/or computer and projector, showing the students how to complete the first part of each new task. Practice all key phrases and words before starting. If the students all say they understand but you are not convinced they do, consider choosing one student to explain what they have to do to the rest of the class.

E

Eating Out with Colleagues

In the west, workplaces sometimes arrange a social outing and then ask around to see who wants to go and leave people to make their own minds up. In Korea things are often done differently. Eating out with colleagues (known as hweh-shik – 회식) is seen as vital in strengthening and maintaining work relationships. Attendance is usually virtually compulsory (excluding genuine emergencies) even when it is announced at the last minute. If people already have other plans or are keen to rush home to their family, they usually have to abandon everything and go along with their fellow workers.*

Public schools tend to have these outings more frequently than academies. Some might not invite their

* I once asked a Korean who worked in a company what would happen if he did not go out with his co-workers. He thought briefly and answered, "Fired!" and started laughing. He probably did not mean it literally but it was clear it could have serious repercussions if he did not go along.

foreign teacher but many will. If the foreign teacher wants to go then that is good. When the foreign teacher does not want to go, some schools might be understanding and accept the differences in western and Korean culture. Others will be less understanding and it could either lead to a deterioration of the relationship between the foreign teacher and the school or as with the Korean teachers, the foreigner may be given very little choice and be made to go one way or another.

Some foreigners will not enjoy these outings, perhaps feeling shy or awkward because of language barriers or uncomfortable with drinking alcohol. Others will enjoy them much more. The food is often very good (and free! – the school or a senior teacher pays) at these events and there may be more chances than at school to get to know colleagues a little better. Even colleagues who cannot speak much English sometimes make more of an effort to start up a conversation, especially after drinking alcohol. It is of course, also a nice chance for foreigners to be brave and attempt to speak some Korean if they have been studying.

After eating at a restaurant, some of the group will often go on to bars or song rooms. It is usually acceptable to go home early after the restaurant and should not cause any problems. It is the not going at all which can make difficulties.

Eleventh Hour Sackings

When foreigners finish a one year contract in Korea they receive severance pay of approximately one month's salary plus a plane ticket or cash equivalent to go home. That is a significant expense for an employer, especially an academy owner. How common it actually was is unclear but there used to be a number of cases of employers, in a bid to escape their contractual obligations, suddenly making a flimsy excuse real or otherwise and sacking the foreigner they had previously seemingly been very happy employing, with about a month to go on his contract i.e. the eleventh month, hence the term 'Eleventh hour sacking'.

Eleventh hour sackings were more of an academy problem than a public school issue. It now happens a lot less [*] mostly because of the Labor Board taking an increasingly tough stance against such courses of action, meaning that it has become much more difficult for the employer to get away with than before. However, the problem has not been totally eliminated and any foreigner who experiences it or suspects it is about to happen should telephone the Labor Board for advice immediately (see page 170).

---

[*] Despite spending several years in Korea, I do not personally know of any foreigners who have come across an eleventh hour sacking either personally or through acquaintances so while it is something worth being aware of, it is not something that should be stressed over.

As ever, prevention is better than cure and sometimes academies that have engaged in such practices in the past end up on one or more of the academy or hagwon blacklists posted on the internet so it is always worth foreigners typing the school or academy name into a search engine and having a quick search before signing a contract in addition to asking targeted questions when given access to the outgoing teacher.

English Names

Many Korean children have English names given to them, especially in their English academies. While the students may have them, they are used less in public schools. If the students do have English names it usually makes it easier for the foreigner to remember the students' names, which is obviously beneficial. It is a good idea to try and learn the students' names as quickly as you can. The teacher's relationship with the students is likely to be better if the teacher knows their names. It should be easier for academy teachers to learn their students' names.

Some of the Korean children may have quite strange English names. In this case, it might be a good idea to ask who chose the name (for example a Korean teacher or a different foreign teacher). If you really think a child has been given a poor deal with the English name he or she has been allocated, you could subtly ask whether the student would like to change the name and suggest a nice alternative but do not try to force a name change on them.

Foreign teachers are sometimes asked to choose English names for new students at an academy either by the workplace or by the children themselves. Take the task seriously.[*] Some students ultimately end up living or studying abroad and using their English name so do not choose something that might get the students laughed at if they live in an English speaking country in the future and try to use their allocated English name as their main name.

Even though many Korean children love to receive English names, do not pressure them into taking an English name if they do not want one, unless the workplace insists they have English names. English names are usually more popular with younger children such as elementary school students and below. Middle and high school students may be less enamoured with the idea of being given an English name and allocating names to them may end up being more trouble than it is worth.

Finally, unlike the Korean children taking English names, foreigners living in Korea do not, under normal circumstances, adopt Korean names!

English Villages

An alternative place to teach English in Korea is at one of the English Villages there. These were designed to

[*] The list of more dubious names I have heard foreign English teachers give children includes 'Orange' and 'Neptune'.

give Korean children extra English immersion without the need to study abroad. They consist of a variety of purpose-built buildings such as post offices, shops, broadcasting stations and so on. Children take part in real-life conversations/role-plays around the village with native English speakers (who may have to dress up in an appropriate uniform) and Korean employees who speak fluent English.

One major difference between working at an English village and a public school or academy is that the students only come to the village for a day or a week so teachers do not get to know the children well. For some teachers, the constant change of students may keep everything fresh but for others it may be seen as a drawback as there is not really any chance to build close or long-lasting relationships with students and to nurture their English ability over time. At most English villages, work is likely to be very similar from day to day or week to week. It will depend on the individual teacher as to whether that is a good or bad point.

F

Fairness

One of the important points a teacher needs to bear in mind is the need to be fair. Under normal circumstances, if Student A is rewarded for doing something, Student B should be if he or she does the same. If Student C is punished for a misdeed and then Student D commits the same offence, Student D should also be punished. If Student E always gets punished for making a lot of noise but is only making a small but troublesome noise today while Student F is always quiet or fairly quiet but is severely disrupting the lesson today then Student F needs punishing first this time. A student's past record should not go in his favour or against him. It sounds simple but it is amazing how often this does not happen and how inconsistent teachers sometimes are.

Teachers need to ensure they give lots of chances to all students to shine and answer questions or volunteer in the classroom. They should avoid choosing the same few students all the time and should also ensure that they give a very similar number of opportunities to male and female students. It is not necessary to keep a running total (although it can be a useful reference to make tallies as one-offs) but it is something to always be conscious of.

The whole idea of fairness and consistency is so important. Students can really resent it if they perceive a teacher (whether rightly or wrongly) to have favourites or prefer one sex of students. If they develop these feelings they are not going to be the most cooperative or enthusiastic of students. It is something a teacher should always guard against.

Follow Through

Many teachers make threats of sanctions, which they then fail to follow through on. By doing this, they risk weakening themselves in the classroom as the students begin to realize that the teacher does not really mean what he says and that they are usually going to be safe to do what they want to do even if the teacher does not want them to.

If a teacher says something like, 'The next person to speak will have to stand in the corner' or 'Any team that leaves any paper on the floor will lose a point,' the teacher needs to follow through on the threat if someone then speaks or one team makes a mess. By consistently applying specified sanctions, the teacher should become stronger in the classroom. If teachers do not want to issue certain sanctions, they need to avoid making threats to do so.

G

Games

Most young students love to play games and they can be an invaluable way of supplementing and consolidating the students' learning. Good games will be highly relevant to current or recent learning or generally suitable to the occasion and will be concerned with giving the students lots of chances to use and put into practice what they have been learning through speaking, listening, reading or writing activities. Some good games will be kinesthetic in nature. Games can be played individually or in teams.

Some games for teaching English may need lots of preparation and organizing but others will not require much at all. Even if students enjoy a particular game, resist the temptation to overuse it. Keep them fresh and only revisit good games once in a while.*

Guessing Games

Korean students love guessing games and the younger they are, the more interested they are. Whether the instructor asks them to guess what is sealed inside a box, what picture is hidden on the other side of a card, or even what the teacher ate for breakfast or lunch, challenging the students to guess an answer is a great way to motivate students and/or introduce new topics or vocabulary. Try to get the students to answer in sentences or to give their guesses in the form of questions. For example if they are guessing what is in the teacher's small bag or box, they could use question structures such as, 'Is it a _______?' or 'Do you have a ________?' Students can be invited to guess answers individually or in groups. If the students are guessing in groups, give them brief discussion time in their groups and then encourage every student in a group to give the answer at the same time using a big voice.

---

* For extensive game ideas see my earlier book '100 Great EFL Games.' (See the back of this book for more information.)

H

Hair Length

Korean middle schools have much stricter rules than elementary schools. This even extends as far as hair length. Female students are not allowed to have long hair in middle school so girls have to cut their hair short towards the end of the sixth and final grade of elementary school or in the holiday before starting middle school, even if they have been growing it long for many years.

Health Insurance

Schools and academies must provide health insurance for their teachers. The employer pays half and the employee pays half, amounting to less than five percent of the teacher's salary. These contributions then entitle foreigners (and their dependents if they have any) to heavily discounted medical treatment. A visit to see a doctor for something such as a heavy cold should not cost more than a few thousand won. Prescription medicines are usually cheap too. Public school contracts always include health insurance. Academies should also provide insurance and thus foreigners should avoid accepting any academy contract which does not offer such a provision.

Heating and Air-Conditioning

Given Korea's climate, workplaces sometimes get extremely hot or very cold. However, that does not guarantee heating or air-conditioning will be used accordingly. Heating a whole school or using air-conditioning to cool one down can be very expensive. Foreigners working in Korean public schools may well find that their school will not switch the heating on until a certain date in the year or until the temperature falls to a predetermined point, no matter how cold it actually feels. Similarly, it may have been hot for a while before there is freedom to use air-conditioning in the summer.

Academies may be even more stringent in the usage they allow. While almost all should use at least some heating in the winter, a small minority of academies may try to avoid using air-conditioning for as much of the summer as possible.* Most should at least use it when it is very hot though and academies that are thriving are likely to use it far more.

Foreigners should be prepared and before heading to Korea they should make sure they pack some very thin summer shirts and some very warm winter clothes which are suitable for the workplace.

---

* The academy I worked in when I first went to Korea only switched the air-conditioning on if they were expecting visits from parents!

I

Inaccurate Books

One of the reasons Koreans make many mistakes with English is surely the quality of some (but not all) of the English study books and children's story books and picture dictionaries available in Korean bookshops. Some books are full of grammatical errors and totally incorrect English sentences and expressions. In many cases it looks like they have been written by Koreans for Koreans without a native speaker ever having checked the books prior to publication. Books designed for self-study or with English and Korean sentences side by side tend to be the worst. If you ever go to a bookshop with Korean friends or acquaintances and they ask you to help choose a good book for studying English from, make sure you meticulously look through a book and check for accuracy for a good few minutes before making a recommendation rather than a quick browse for a few seconds.

Induction

Some foreigners no doubt arrive at a Korean school or academy for the first time expecting a proper induction and a period of being eased into their new position. For those that have a signed a contract with one of the major government sponsored programmes to work in a public school starting at the beginning of March or September (i.e. the start of one of Korea's two semesters) a full induction should be forthcoming during the week or so before starting work. Foreigners who are hired out of season or without going through the official government programmes are much less likely to have an induction although some training opportunities may or may not be provided periodically later on. Public school inductions are also a good opportunity for meeting other new teachers and making a few friends.

For new teachers arriving at academies, things are less predictable. A short period of shadowing the outgoing teacher teaching his or her classes lasting anything from a day or two up to about a week is possible. Sometimes though, the academy will expect their new teachers to go straight into the classroom and teach, even if they have no prior teaching experience.

Given the unpredictability of what kind of induction or training will be provided, foreign teachers really need to have done some homework before heading to Korea. A qualification such as TESOL (Teaching English to Speakers of Other Languages) is certainly handy, although a full qualification might take a few weeks and cost a significant chunk of money to obtain. At the very least, new teachers should try and read some books related to EFL (English as a Foreign Language) which provide some theory, methods and ideas for how to organize lessons and some useful activities and games. Buying a couple of books of photocopiable activities to take to Korea is also a good idea. Finally, new teachers should talk to any friends that may have taught EFL in the past, even if they taught in countries other than Korea. What advice can they pass on? What worked well for them? What did they find difficult?

International Schools (2)

The continuous expansion in the number of international schools in Korea offers a further employment option for foreign teachers. However, under normal circumstances a teacher cannot simply make the switch from teaching English as a Foreign Language to working in an international school and teaching classes closely or loosely based on western curriculums.

To teach in an international school in Korea, the absolute minimum requirement is normally a teacher license from one's own country.* Most schools will also ask for at least two years post qualification teaching experience in the teacher's home country. For the top schools even more experience than that might be necessary to be competitive during recruitment cycles. A Masters Degree is useful to have too although not usually essential as is some experience in EFL environments. Being a dedicated Christian and able to prove it might also be an advantage for gaining employment at some schools.

---

* If they are not asking for this, they may not have any accreditation or they may even be an English language academy (hagwon) with a misleading name.

Many teachers are interviewed and selected in their own country. Recruitment cycles usually begin in the winter ahead of a September start. Teaching couples often fair well and are commonly employed together. Even if a school is teaching an American curriculum, qualified teachers from Britain, Canada, Australia and so on are able to apply and similarly if a school is teaching a British curriculum, American teachers and those of other nationalities may seek employment.

Teachers who accept jobs to teach in international schools in Korea will need a visa. The school will help with this. Unlike the English academies and Korean public schools which only employ foreign teachers on one year contracts, many international schools offer two year contracts. If teachers have children, many schools will let at least one or two children study at the school free but it is important to check this out before committing to a contract.

Some of the low end international schools in Korea might not pay any more than academy jobs despite the much more demanding workload. However, the stronger schools should pay a better salary (often significantly so) on a scale which is commensurate with experience. They will usually have good additional benefits which may include some or all of the following; generous relocation allowances, career personal development allowances, annual or end of contract airplane tickets for the whole family, good sized accommodation and of course the fee waiver for the teacher's children, which represents a huge saving.

Internet Forums

There are a few internet forums devoted to teaching in South Korea. People planning to visit or move to Korea sometimes use them to ask questions they may have about teaching and work conditions or aspects of Korean life. Others may use them to discuss situations they are encountering while in Korea. While these forums often provide people with all sorts of useful information, they sometimes contain a lot of negativity giving a somewhat distorted image of Korea. If you use these forums, keep an open mind. Remember that there are usually two sides to every story. Also bear in mind that a lot more people go on to such forums to let off steam and complain than people who go on to write about what a good day they have just had.

K

Korean Speaking?

One common question family members may ask when someone announces they are going to Korea to teach English is, 'How are you going to teach Korean children if you can't speak Korean?' The person in question may well wonder the same thing and whether he or she should learn some Korean very quickly to help teach the students. In short, it is not necessary and there are a number of reasons why this is the case.

If the foreign teacher can speak Korean and the students know about it, some students will sometimes either give up trying to speak English and just talk in only Korean, or speak English when it is easy for them but then revert back to Korean the moment the vocabulary gets more challenging and takes them out of their comfort zone. Similarly when it comes to listening to the teacher, some students will stop concentrating hard and will wait for the foreign teacher to explain in Korean whether it be well or at a simple level. The net result of a foreigner using Korean can potentially be a serious decrease in the speed the Korean students improve their English listening and speaking skills. Similarly this can be an issue in a team-teaching situation if the Korean teacher insists on translating everything that the foreign teacher says into Korean and should be discouraged where possible.

If the foreign teacher cannot speak Korean (or the students do not think that he or she can), the students are challenged more. If they cannot say or explain something in English, they are forced to use alternative strategies such as trying to think of another way of saying what they want to say, using body language in addition to broken English or even drawing a picture to emphasize a point. By overcoming such challenges successfully, students develop confidence that serves them well in the future. One possibility for consolidating this even further is to use a no

Korean policy in the classroom (see page 184).

It may well be that it is not just the students who are challenged more if Korean is not used in the classroom. The foreign teacher may also hit points when he says something and no-one understands even if he repeats it, but just as students overcome challenges to improve their English skills, the teacher must also tackle such obstacles to become a more skilled teacher by learning how to explain concepts better or in a simpler way.*

In some teaching situations in Korea, whether it be in a public school or academy, one common scenario is for the foreign teacher to teach a topic or area first and for the children to have a class with a Korean teacher at a later date who then reviews key points, using Korean if deemed necessary to increase students' understanding. Therefore it really should not be necessary for the foreign teacher to use Korean in the classroom.

---

* If this proves problematic, teachers should consider investing in a few quality books or even completing qualifications such as a TESOL qualification (Teaching English to Speakers of Other Languages). More experienced teachers can look into a Masters Degree or Delta qualification amongst others to help them teach more complicated concepts in English such as grammar.

L

Labor Board

In the relatively rare case that foreigners in Korea have major contractual disputes with their employer that have been impossible to solve through dialogue or help from other people, the ultimate step is to contact the Korean Labor Board. To contact them, call 1350. They are open Monday to Friday and have English speakers available.

Lack of Communication

One issue many foreigners find themselves dealing with at various points while they work in Korea is the failure of co-workers or superiors to issue information that most people would deem as essential. There are occasions where foreign teachers may find themselves turning up to empty classrooms or if they have their own classroom, a class not showing up when Korean teachers have forgotten to relay changes to the schedule or important events that the foreigner should have been made aware of in advance.

This lack of communication can be extremely frustrating for foreign teachers, especially if they have spent a lot of time preparing for a lesson. However, getting angry and confronting Korean co-workers for their failure to pass on important information is unlikely to be helpful. Instead a decisive sounding, 'Please let me know next time,' is likely to be more beneficial, possibly adding that you spent a lot of time preparing for the lesson.

Also remember that once the initial frustration of not being informed about a cancelled lesson subsides, you have got a bit of bonus time to use for preparing other lessons or even to have a quick cup of coffee or tea and relax for a few minutes, and in most situations your earlier efforts will not go to waste as you can still teach the lesson you had already planned at a later date.

Language Exchanges

Finding a Korean friend who will teach you Korean free while you give English classes for nothing in return sounds like the perfect arrangement all round. There are plenty of such arrangements around. However, even in this situation foreigners should tread a little bit carefully. Even if money does not change hands, this kind of private English lesson is still technically violating a foreign teacher's visa.

In reality, the chances of running into trouble for doing a language exchange must be pretty minimal.* If a foreign English teacher and a Korean are having a conversation class in a coffee shop or somewhere similar, it would be pretty difficult to prove they were not just friends enjoying a coffee and chat together unless they were sat

---

* I have never heard of a case of someone getting into trouble with immigration under these circumstances but there is no room for complacency. The note of caution being relayed here is something that does come up occasionally.

there with a table full of notebooks, pens and English conversation or grammar books...

Last Minute

One thing that upsets foreigners in Korea from time to time is the very last minute nature of Korean society, whether it is saving work until it is almost too late or waiting until there are only a few minutes to go or even literally the final moment to announce something such as a compulsory/near-compulsory dinner with your school teachers.* The reasons can be one from many. Some Koreans are just so busy, they do not have time to do everything or their busyness makes them forget important matters like relaying crucial information to their foreign teachers. Sometimes it may just be that something a foreigner would deem critical or highly beneficial to know significantly in advance is not considered so important by a Korean. Other times, the decision is not actually made until the last second. It is not always like this of course but neither is it an uncommon occurrence. It surely happens more in Korea than in the average workplace in your home country.

If you become a 'victim' of this practice, becoming

* This happens in both public schools and academies. In an academy I remember being told about new classes at three o'clock at literally one minute's notice (2:59), while in a public school I have been told of work dinners just minutes from normal going home time.

openly angry is unlikely to be useful even if you are fuming inside. It might help to bear in mind that it is not just you it is happening to. Again the better course of action is a decisive sounding, 'Please let me know next time.' That sometimes works for a while but do not be surprised to see old habits return at a later date!

Learn from the Students

Teachers often explain and demonstrate an activity, give the students the go ahead to start, and then begin to walk around the classroom to monitor, observe and additionally guide students when necessary. While doing that, teachers sometimes spot students doing the task differently to how it was outlined either due to misunderstandings or on rare occasions because they have taken it upon themselves to change an activity because they think their way is better or more interesting!

In this situation the teacher should try to avoid immediately halting the students and ordering them back to the intended method and should instead just stop to pause and observe for a brief time. Use the students' misconceptions to aid with planning a similar lesson in the future. Occasionally, the students own version of an activity, which has emerged from misunderstanding or their own interpretation of an activity, actually turns out to be an improvement on the teacher's version or at least a viable future alternative. Sometimes the new method enables students to use the target language better or perhaps to practise it as much as before but with tweaks to the activity that make it more interesting or exciting overall. Always try to be open-minded.

Learning Goal

Each lesson should have a clearly defined learning goal. The aim should not just be that the students will study pages 36 and 37 of their textbooks today. It should be something more specific and language related such as learning how to ask and answer a certain target question or talking about their daily life. Many teachers will write the goal of the lesson on the board in simple language or show it using Microsoft PowerPoint at the beginning of a lesson and go through it with the students so that they know the purpose of the lesson. If students know what they are trying to achieve, they will generally focus better.

Leaving Korea

Coming to the end of a contract and preparing to head home is a time of mixed emotions with excitement of seeing friends and family again combined with various feelings about leaving Korea. It is also often a slightly stressful time with plane tickets to organise, money to send home and so on. Occasionally workplaces tell their native teacher that they will send the severance pay to their home bank account after they have finished their contract. It is probably not a good idea to accept this if an academy proposes it. The teacher should insist on getting the money paid before leaving. This system happens a bit more often in public schools although it is probably still the exception rather than the rule. Unlike academies, they can usually be trusted to send the money on.

Leaving Work Early

Workers around the world often find themselves in situations where they could do with leaving work early to deal with some personal business such as banking or a trip to the post office. For most teachers in Korea, this should not be a problem. Academy teachers who start work in the afternoon have the mornings to take care of what needs doing, such as sending money back to their own country. For academy teachers teaching kindergarten, it might be a bit more of a problem but in most situations there should be a small gap somewhere during the week for the teacher to nip out for half an hour or so to do what needs doing.

Public schools are usually very reasonable about teachers occasionally leaving an hour or so early at the end of the day, providing no classes or other important duties are compromised. It usually involves a foreign teacher telling one of the Korean English teachers and then signing a document, which will also be signed by other people such as the vice-principal. The Korean word for leaving early is 조퇴 (jo-tay).

Lesson Planning

Some Korean academies and schools expect their

foreign teachers to submit lesson plans in advance while others do not. Even if there are no such obligations, teachers really should consider making a lesson plan of some sort for each class. It can be difficult to find the time to do this if teaching a large number of unique classes each week but often it will be the case that more than one class will study the same pages in a book or the same topic in a given week. Even when they do not, other classes will sometimes do the same lesson a few months later or at a similar time the following year. Gradually a teacher can put together files of lesson plans and resources which can be invaluable, convenient and save time later on.

Lesson plans are valuable for ensuring each class has a focus (i.e. a learning goal for the students to achieve – see page 174), clear directions for how the students are going to achieve the target of the lesson and the means for checking they have understood and succeeded. They also help teachers maintain their composure and poise if they momentarily forget something important, encounter something unexpected in the class or just generally feel under a bit of pressure. It is perfectly acceptable for teachers to place a lesson plan on their desk at the front of the classroom and catch a brief glimpse of it mid-lesson.[*] Additionally a lesson plan does not have to be rigorously followed one hundred percent. It is usually fine for teachers

---

[*] However, do not spend too much time studying it during a class otherwise teaching becomes awkward and unnatural.

to respond to something that happens in a lesson or make adjustments if suddenly hit by a moment of inspiration.

Lesson plans may contain brief or more detailed information about the activities that will be used in a class, timings for how much time will be allocated for each activity, how the students will be organized (i.e. individual work, in pairs, small groups etc.), what resources will be used (textbooks, worksheets, word or picture cards, games, computer files, video clips, songs, puppets, colour pens, blindfolds etc.), whether any provisions will be made for high or low level students such as differentiation of tasks by level or additional support and so on.

After completing a lesson, good teachers will sometimes make some brief notes on their lesson plan sheet(s) or a separate piece of paper about how the lesson went, how the students fared, any problems that occurred, anything else that was unexpected and any ideas for changes to the lesson if teaching the same topic again in the future. Occasionally teachers may even keep samples or photocopies of students work from a given lesson to refer back to and to inform future planning.

Of course, no matter how well a teacher plans a lesson, things will occasionally happen that throw a lesson totally off course. Students may find an activity much easier or more difficult than the teacher expected, they may respond to one part of a lesson with far more or less enthusiasm than predicted or completely misunderstand an activity and do it in a way the teacher has not expected, whether for better or for worse. Computers sometimes suddenly develop problems or start a go-slow. For example the important file containing a PowerPoint presentation for the students to learn from which the teacher successfully tested on the classroom computer before the lesson suddenly does not open at the crucial time.

There are so many possible variables of what could happen in a classroom. When something does go wrong, the teacher without a plan is the one who usually struggles or panics the most and ends up standing in the classroom wondering what on earth to do next. This can even be the case when nothing terrible occurs. Unprepared teachers are likely to have times where they get stuck mid-class or finish a class much too early and run out of activities. The teacher who has planned a lesson carefully is much better equipped to respond to the unexpected and quickly move on to another activity instead or begin a Plan B.

Letters of Recommendation

Many Korean workplaces ask for letters of recommendation when recruiting teachers. Public schools may accept letters from previous employers and former university professors. Teachers looking to move into university employment in Korea are likely to need one or more letters from previous employers (ideally teaching roles) and often as many as three. Whenever foreigners leave a teaching job in Korea on good terms with their employer, it is a good idea to ask for a letter detailing time worked and a short overview of how they are a good teacher. Foreigners should also ask for each letter to be stamped. These letters can be very useful for getting a better job in the future.

Letter of Release

When foreign teachers in Korea on a regular E visa want to change jobs while under contract either because their current position is not working out well or because they have found a better job elsewhere, they must obtain a letter of release from their employer. This document needs to be stamped by the employer and then it should be taken to the local immigration office. Note that some employers, especially academy directors, are likely to refuse to sign the document.

Lunch

For many foreigners working in English academies, they will not start work until early afternoon. However, if the academy includes a kindergarten, the foreigner will usually have the opportunity to eat lunch at the academy. Public school teachers will obviously work through the day and be at school at lunch time. Standard lunchtime fare is usually some rice accompanied by some kind of soup (which on occasions may be a quite watery kind of soup), a small sprinkling of side dishes (mainly various kinds of vegetables but sometimes a little bit of meat too) and last but not least, kimchi of course.

Do foreign teachers have to eat at their workplace? While some academies may insist, many are likely to allow the foreign teachers to eat elsewhere if they wish. Public schools are much more likely to insist the foreign teacher stays at the school as they are responsible for the teacher for the whole day and could face problems if he or she leaves the school at lunchtime and is subsequently unlucky enough to have an accident of some sort.

M

Midnight Runner

Occasionally a foreigner runs into serious problems at a Korean workplace and rightly or wrongly decides that the only answer is to runaway or suddenly disappear.* An expatriate who follows such a path in Korea is known as a midnight runner. Foreigners who do this, usually wait until they receive their monthly salary and then get on a plane

---

* How often this happens in reality is not clear. There are a few stories around of midnight runners but I do not personally know anyone who knows anyone else who did a midnight runner. Anyway, you never know who might end up on the plane with you – when I was once going back to England for a visit, one of my students ended up taking the same bus to the airport and then followed me all the way to Hong Kong before we changed planes to our final destinations!

out of the country either within approximately twenty-fours or at the following weekend. If things are particularly bad, they may not even wait to get paid and just go sooner. This sometimes happens when foreigners give in their notice and then become convinced they are going to be swindled out of money from their final payday.

Midnight runners are generally more likely to work at academies than at public schools. Sometimes the problems foreigners perceive themselves as having can be solved or at least reduced through dialogue with their employer or with the assistance of co-workers. If that fails, they can try their recruiter who placed them in the academy or their local education office that placed them in a public school. Some of these people will be helpful and able to improve a situation but others might not be – it will vary. The Labor Board (see page 170) is sometimes able to act in the case of severe contract breaches.

If help does not seem to be forthcoming, it is probably understandable that some people do not know what to do next and feel very vulnerable, angry or even scared especially as they are so far from home. These feelings are probably what make people contemplate running away. Whether it is morally right to do so is subjective and certain to divide opinion.

When a foreigner does a midnight runner after work one day or in the early hours of the following day, usually the first thing the employer knows is when the teacher does not show up for work the next day and proves impossible to contact because he or she is already on a plane back home. If however, the employer finds out in time, gets tipped off or already has an inkling, it might be possible for them to contact immigration which could then pose problems for the foreigner at the airport attempting to leave.

The consequences of a midnight run are potentially dire all round. For the runner, it might feel good or a relief at first but it has to be assumed that for some that would soon turn into feelings of guilt which could linger for a long time afterwards. For the employer, it might take a few weeks to find a new teacher. In the case of an academy, it could cost them a lot of money, not only to find a new teacher but from a possible loss of students if the parents are unhappy because there are suddenly fewer foreign teachers there. Fellow workers will also suffer a lot too, especially in smaller workplaces. Everyone will have to teach several extras classes for a while to cover the runaway teacher, increasing workload significantly. It can also be unsettling for the students too. In short, a midnight runner lets a lot of people down.

Multiple Schools

Some foreign public school teachers through the government sponsored schemes in Korea end up signing contracts, which see them working at more than one school. Occasionally they may even work at more than two schools.

Foreign teachers working at multiple schools may be entitled to an additional allowance of between 100,000 won and 150,000 won. Some foreign teachers like the little bit of extra salary but others note the inconvenience of moving around so much during the week and not being at one school long enough to build very strong relationships with the students as drawbacks.

Foreign teachers working at English academies will ordinarily be employed by one academy only. If the foreigner needs to work at two academies, this should be clearly stated in the contract before signing.* After arriving at Korea, both academies need registering with the immigration office even if they are different branches of the same chain otherwise the foreign teacher will be working illegally.

In the very unlikely event that an academy suddenly tries to make a foreign teacher work at a second place in mid–contract, the foreigner should ideally refuse and stand his or her ground pointing out that he or she came to work at one academy only. If the academy persists, the foreign

* Even if it is clearly stated, it is a definite potential red flag and a reason for not signing. It is quite possible that it could be legitimate but a significant chance that something is not going to be quite right. There are many other jobs out there where you will only work at one academy so do not be pressured into signing something that does not seem quite right.

teacher should try contacting the recruiter that placed him or her in the first place. If that does not bear fruit, the teacher must make absolutely certain that the new workplace is also added at the immigration office to make it legal. If the academy will not do that, it may be time to consider handing in your notice or to contact the Labor Board (see page 170) to see if they can help you.

N

No Korean!

Some teachers may try and enforce a no Korean speaking policy during English classes. Students are prohibited from speaking in Korean to the teacher or to their friends, whether it be off-topic and unrelated to the lesson or genuinely trying to help a friend with some explanation or translation in Korean. No Korean approaches may cover a whole academy building in an extreme case but more commonly will be applied to a school or academy English classroom. Sometimes there may even be just one section of a classroom or a large open area which is allocated to be an English Zone, where only English may be spoken. Rules for the exclusive use of English tend to just cover actual lesson times and not immediately before or after classes although there may be exceptions.

In theory, totally banning the students' first

language in English classes should be beneficial in pushing the children to challenge themselves to communicate in English. In practice, it can be more difficult. If teaching English in a country such as America or England, where the learners are likely to come from several countries, students will not often be able to speak each other's first language meaning that they are forced to communicate in English and are likely to reap the rewards of this. However, if a native teacher is teaching in the students' own country such as Korea, all students will be able to talk in their first language and many will regularly do so.

Policing a no Korean policy in a classroom can be very difficult or even stressful. Should minor student lapses back into Korean be ignored? What about if students continue to frequently speak Korean? Should they be punished in some way? If students are able to go whole lessons without speaking any Korean should they be rewarded? And if so, how? It may raise more questions than it answers.

The decision as to whether to forbid the use of students' first language in a classroom is a tricky one and it is an issue which often sparks fierce debate. In classes where students really embrace a ban and show very positive attitudes to an English only approach, the rewards can be great with strong student progress. It may even have behavioural benefits too.[*] On the other hand, as long as the students study well most of the time and overall progress is at a respectable rate, does it matter if a bit of Korean is heard from time to time during a lesson? There is no definitive answer and different teachers will have alternative views. Inexperienced teachers may want to experiment with banning Korean either with certain classes or for one-off lessons or parts of lessons to form their own opinions.

No Sick Days?

Foreigners working in Korea sometimes come into conflict with their employer through their use of sick days. Most Korean workers tend not to use sick days unless they are really sick or hospitalized, even if this means spreading germs around the workplace. Similarly, student attendance in public schools always seems to be very high.[†] All of this

[*] I had one particularly noisy and misbehaving but capable class during my first ever year of teaching. I introduced a no Korean rule for these students. I told them they could speak as much as they liked, as long as they only spoke in English. They accepted it really well, spoke lots of English to each other even when unprompted and their behaviour greatly improved too.

[†] Other than the Swine Flu outbreak in 2009, it was always more common than not for the whole class to be present during my several years teaching at a Korean elementary school whereas when I taught in England 100% student attendance was comparatively rare.

means that many Koreans struggle to understand when and if foreigners phone in sick. Also, the number of permitted sick days in a contract is often low and just because they are there does not mean they are particularly designed to be used.

If foreign workers are lucky, they will work somewhere that is very understanding when they need time off sick. If they are less lucky, it could lead to problems such as the sick days being taken off holiday allowances, co-workers being sent round to their house to check up on them etc. These examples are extreme and rare but have been known to happen. They are more likely to happen in language academies where it is difficult to cover for sick teachers, especially at short notice.*

It is not unusual in public schools, for sick teachers (including the Korean teachers) to force themselves to go to work, teach all their classes and then get permission to go home early to rest i.e. take a jo-tay (조퇴) – see page 175. This is likely to make a better impression than just taking a whole day off sick.

---

* I personally did not have any problems on the very rare occasions that I needed to use sick days. My friends did not have any issues either. However, back in my hagwon days, one of my Korean co-workers had to deal with unpleasantness after phoning in sick for the second time in the space of a few months.

O

'Old' Teachers

Slightly older people, as opposed to those who have graduated in recent times, often wonder whether they can get a job teaching in Korea. The short answer is yes, providing they fulfill the visa requirements. However, the older a person is, the harder it may prove to get a job. Many academies will prefer their teachers to be young (ideally recent graduates or if not, certainly not much older than thirty). Some will be less selective than others so some older teachers should be able to find a job if they are patient.

Public schools are slightly different and sometimes employ teachers in their forties, fifties and occasionally beyond.* Well-qualified, mature applicants may sometimes have more joy applying to Korean universities. International school jobs in Korea are also definitely worth exploring for teachers with extensive experience of teaching in primary or secondary schools in their own country.

Open Class

Just as teachers in their own country may get observed teaching by colleagues or superiors once in a while, classes are sometimes opened up for outsiders in Korea.

---

* For instance, the website of EPIK (English Program in Korea) suggested any applicants under the age of sixty-two would be considered for the autumn 2012 public school teacher intake.

As a foreigner working in an academy, any open class is likely to be for parents to come and watch. In public schools, classes may be opened up for parents, fellow teachers, education officials or even student teachers if the school has them. The average public school will have more open classes per year than the average academy. Korean public school teachers have to be observed a certain number of times per year so foreign teachers are likely to have open English classes team-teaching with a Korean teacher at various points. Foreigners in academies may not have any open classes at all if they are lucky. Even if the academy does have open classes they will probably only run once or twice a year.

Open classes may sound daunting and they can certainly be nerve-wracking but with good preparation, the chances of a successful class are favourable. Many students are good all or most of the time anyway but with an audience watching their every move, even students whose attitude may sometimes be called into question tend to be much more focused and positive than normal! If parents are watching, some students will want to show off their ability. Conversely, other students will suddenly go very shy and not want to answer or present anything.

Many public school open classes are essentially all about the Korean teacher, even in English class. Regardless of what the normal class role of the foreign teacher is, whether it be teaching almost all of the lesson alone, teaching split down the middle or the Korean teacher dominating, it is likely that the Korean teacher will prepare all or most of the open class lesson materials alone (but often after a consultation or a sharing of ideas with the foreign teacher) and teach more of the open class than the foreign teacher or an equal amount at the very least. Foreign teacher dominated open classes are rare in public schools unless it is an afterschool class taught only by the foreign teacher. Consequently the Korean teacher is likely to get most of the praise if the class is successful and should take responsibility if it is not great. Occasionally, the success or failure of an open class may have some impact on whether the foreign teacher's contract is renewed.

Open classes should not be seen as a deterrent against going to teach in South Korea.* As noted before, they are not a regular occurrence, especially in academies. Also, it is rare for open classes to be disastrous failures and very normal for them to be satisfactory or better and often as good as if not better than a regular class. Many open classes have some element of 'stage-management' to them. Classes will often warm up with an English song the children already know particularly well and the main activity or activities in the class are often ones the students have done before for different topics so that they are fully

* After all, almost all jobs across all industries have some sort of ongoing employee monitoring, assessments, targets, appraisals, annual reports etc.

familiar with the methods involved. It is rare to introduce massive amounts of new vocabulary. Consolidating what the students already know is more common. If parents are watching, most will not be educational experts and will not have explicit professional knowledge of what constitutes a good lesson. If the children (especially their own child) look happy and are successfully using a bit of English, the chances are most of them will go away happy.

P

Parents

Korean parents are incredibly passionate about their children's education with many spending several hundred pounds or dollars each month and in some cases even more than that for their children to take extra classes at academies and other places. Some also hire private tutors. Obviously they expect good results on their investment in the way of very, very high grades for their children and ultimately a highly regarded university. This puts real pressure on some children for whom even 99% in a test can be seen as a failure in worse-case scenarios.

At some academies, parents are able to wield quite a lot of power as they are paying customers. If they are not happy, they can easily move their child and their money to a rival academy, which most academy owners will be eager to avoid. They can also spread the word to any other parents they are friendly with. This means that academy owners will often take steps to appease parents and may make concessions to parental demands. The smaller and more vulnerable and volatile the number of students, the more power the parents are likely to be able to exert.

At public schools, many parents enjoy strong relationships with the teachers. Parental committees are well-represented. Most parents will be very respectful to their child's teacher(s) and if there is some kind of problem with their child at school, they are more likely to support or acknowledge the teacher than challenge or argue with him or her.

A minority of Korean parents significantly overestimate or underestimate their child's academic ability or potential. Some will think their significantly below average child is the next Einstein while others will consider their child who is second or third in the class for most subjects to be a struggler. Handling such situations with tact is very important.

Foreigners teaching English in Korea are not likely to come into very regular contact with parents. Some parents will be very scared or nervous of trying to communicate with foreign teachers! Seeing them and exchanging hellos in English or Korean is not unusual but more meaningful interaction is less common. A few parents speak English better and sometimes try to engage foreign teachers in more meaningful conversations, while others may approach foreigners more if they know the foreigner has some proficiency in Korean. They will usually be friendly.

Pay and Savings Potential

One of Korea's many attractions for foreign teachers is the opportunity it offers for saving money. In terms of savings potential, it is renowned for being one of the best countries for teachers with few or no specialist qualifications for teaching English (excluding the compulsory degree certification) to go and teach and save money. While some teachers find countries such as China, Thailand or Japan more appealing, Korea compares favourably from a financial viewpoint. It pays respectably, has low taxation and foreigners who do not live too extravagantly frequently mention being able to save around half of their salary and in some cases a fair bit more than that.

Paying Off Student Loans

Foreigners frequently go to South Korea to teach almost immediately after graduating. One of the biggest reasons for this is to try and pay off a significant chunk of their student loans. It is very common to hear of people successfully accomplishing this goal during their time in Korea (sometimes more than a single twelve month contract) due to the savings potential Korea offers. England's student loan repayment system differs to those in

America and Canada for example so graduates from England may not make a significant impression on paying back their loan without making voluntary overpayments. People from England should note however, that repayments take place at a lower threshold when working in South Korea (or many other countries for that matter) than they do while in England, taking into account differences in average salaries and living costs.

Pay Rise

Often foreigners have a happy and successful year and look to extend their contract by another year. When they come to negotiating and signing another twelve month contract the expectation of a pay rise is understandable, especially now that they have more experience. Unfortunately this is not always forthcoming.

Public schools usually have a salary scale to follow (especially if they are employing foreign teachers through one of the major government programmes), which sets out the pay for each level of experience based on the number of years taught with some recognition given for certain qualifications. This should ensure pay rises each or most years although a foreigner can get stuck if they make it to the top of the scale.

Language academies are less predictable. Some may increase foreign teacher salaries at each renewal and occasionally by more than a public school would, others may just do so once every two or three years while the rest may never do so as long as the teacher stays. Sometimes, academy teachers negotiate a slight increase in their holiday allowance instead of a pay rise.

The most common pay rise is 100,000 won per month although occasionally it can be 200,000 won. On rare occasions, rises of 50,000 won or 150,000 won per month may be given.

Reasons employers may be reluctant to give rises may include that they are genuinely short of money or are content with their worker but not so much that they are willing to pull out all the stops to keep them. More commonly though, is the fact that there are always new people looking to come and teach in South Korea who would be more than willing to work at the same salary or even a lower one than their current teacher is working at. The irony of this is that not only can it often be very expensive for public schools or academies to find new teachers (unless they happen to be lucky enough to know or have links to a teacher who could replace an outgoing teacher) but also the outgoing teacher will have gained one or more years experience and therefore be likely to teach better than the fresh teacher that comes in. *

---

* If they end up having to use a recruiter to find a new foreign teacher, it can sometimes cost almost as much, if not more than, the annual cost of giving a teacher a pay rise of 100,000 won per month.

If a foreign teacher cannot get the pay rise he or she is looking for, a difficult decision has to be made. If the teacher has done a good job, it should be quite easy to move to a new workplace or perhaps even try applying to a university. However, Korean workplaces are very unpredictable so this may not always be the best choice. As with a first job in Korea, any potential new jobs should be investigated with great care and diligence before committing to them. In some cases staying put, even without a pay rise, may actually be the best bet for the time being. If the foreigner was happy throughout the contract with the exception of not being offered a pay rise, it might be worth trying to seek some benefits elsewhere in the new contract such as increased holidays in an academy or exploring the possibility for more overtime classes in a public school. These will not always be forthcoming but may be worth a try.

Pension

While teaching English in Korea, employees should have pension contributions deducted from their salary which are then matched by the employer. For those working in public schools and universities, this should be automatic. American, Canadian and Australian teachers have the option of claiming both their own and their employer's contributions back in a lump sum when they leave Korea, which can amount to a significant figure.

Unfortunately this does not currently extend to teachers from New Zealand, Britain and Ireland, nor is there a system in place for transferring payments made back to one's own country upon leaving Korea.

Academy owners often ignore their obligations and avoid paying pension and do not make any deductions from their workers (not just from foreign teachers but from their Korean teachers too). For teachers from New Zealand, Britain and Ireland, this is not necessarily such a bad thing for the reasons outlined above as long as the academy is trustworthy in other regards.

The lack of pension for English teachers from certain countries can be a sore point for some but it does not necessarily need to be a deal-breaker or the trigger to give South Korea a miss and go and teach in another country instead. Even without the pension arrangements, many foreign teachers find South Korea favourable from a financial perspective, especially with regards to savings potential.

Personalization of Learning

Textbooks for teaching English come in all kinds of formats. Particularly at elementary school level, books may centre around reappearing characters, either animated or real people. Hopefully your students will be interested in these characters. In some cases however, students will become bored of the characters, if their interest was ever roused in the first place. Books with no recurring characters, whether they be at high, middle or even elementary school level, all share a common characteristic. The students feel little or no connection to the people that dialogues and key learning points are based around, which does little to stimulate their curiosity.

One way to motivate students and make their study more meaningful is through the personalization of learning. This can be done in various ways. Examples include putting the names of students or teachers at the school on to activity sheets. If the students are studying about sport, hobbies or other activities, assess their understanding by making a worksheet which requires the students to read and draw* appropriate pictures. If the names of the students in a class include Yunji, Sumin, Hyunseo and Minsu, type or write sentences such as, 'Yunji likes to play tennis and Sumin likes to play soccer,' 'Hyunseo can't play tennis well' or 'Minsu will play baseball at two o'clock.'

Another good way to make students' learning more personal and relevant is to present learning content using slideshows on Microsoft PowerPoint or your preferred choice of software if you have the means to display your computer screen somewhere in the classroom i.e. on a large screen, television, interactive whiteboard etc. Use photos of students and/or teachers at your workplace in slideshows

---

* See 'Artistic' on page 121 for a note on Korean children and art.

on Microsoft PowerPoint and ask students to make or practise sentences or questions and answers for what they see.

Personalization can be very motivating for the students but as with any technique, activity or game which works well, do not overdo it by using it in virtually every lesson or the effects and benefits will begin to wear off.

Phasing Out?

It has been a long-stated aim for South Korea to get their public school teachers up to a level of English proficiency that will make it unnecessary to employ any foreign teachers in elementary, middle or high schools. This is sought both as a cost-cutting measure, as employing foreign teachers is a considerable expense, and also for the development of Korean people and their ability to learn and use English effectively.

Lee Myung-bak (Korean president 2008~2012) caused a major storm when he proposed that all schools should teach all classes in English by 2010. Following strong opposition this idea was abandoned. Korean elementary school student teachers now have to pass a short English teaching demonstration at the end of their course before they can qualify. Amongst other initiatives, robot English teachers have been trialed including the experiments in Daegu that started in 2010.*

Clearly, South Korea has some big ideas to improve skills and reduce dependence on native English teachers but this goal has not yet become a reality despite periods of uncertainty over the future of foreign teachers in Korean schools. One dramatic development came in 2011, when it was announced that most foreign public high school English teachers in Seoul would not have their contracts renewed nor would they be replaced. Elsewhere though, foreign teachers are still continuing to get jobs in public schools, especially in elementary schools. The end does not yet seem nigh.

Even if Korean government sponsored programmes for recruiting native English teachers were brought to an end, some wealthier schools might still be able to find and recruit teachers themselves, if their budget allows it. Parental pressure could ensure they do. Regardless of what happens with public schools, it is highly likely that foreign teachers will still be around in Korea. Unless legislation is passed to prevent it, expect English academies to continue to employ foreign teachers for a long time yet.

Photos (2)

In some countries the practice of asking for a photo

---

* Ironically, these robots had to be externally controlled by Filipino teachers.

to be included with a job application would be frowned upon but for jobs in Korea it can be an important part of the selection process. Unfortunately but inevitably it opens up the possibility of discrimination.* Before applying for a teaching job in South Korea it is vital to get a very good photo taken, preferably while wearing professional clothes. Occasionally applicants may also wish to include one or more photos of them successfully working with children and everyone looking happy.

Plaster Casts

Any teacher spending some time teaching students in Korea is likely to notice just how often Korean students seem to get hurt. The frequency of students coming to school or an academy with a plaster cast, using bandages or having other signs of a physical injury seems to be far higher than in western schools. Why this should be the case is not clear but usually it would be very wrong to suspect anything sinister happening to the students. Perhaps surprisingly considering its popularity in Korea, it is very rare for the injuries to be taekwondo-related. When asking students what happened, common replies include, 'I hurt it

---

* One strange form of discrimination that may sporadically exist is against facial hair. Koreans do not often grow beards or even moustaches. If bearded applicants find themselves getting continuously turned down, it may be worth experimenting by temporarily shaving the beard off and taking a new clean-shaven photo to submit with applications. The beard can always be grown back at a later date.

playing soccer,' 'I fell over in the playground' and 'I fell down or tripped on some stairs at school.' It seems safe to conclude that Korean students are accident-prone or just plain unlucky![*]

Positive Reinforcement

Almost all teachers have to deal with student behavioural issues at various stages. For some teachers this can be a major source of stress, especially if the methods they use to deal with problems fail or seem to have negligible effect. Inexperienced teachers are often far too negative with their approach to these situations, constantly saying (or sometimes shouting) something like, 'Minsu, don't X', 'Minsu, don't Y' and 'Minsu, don't Z'. They may also send Minsu out of the classroom or make him sit or stand in a corner almost every other lesson.

Despite various kinds of warnings or punishments, some students never appear to change their behaviour. Some may even seem to be amused by being punished, especially if other students laugh along. To stop or at least significantly reduce the frequency of these situations,

---

[*] As if to prove this point, one of my Korean co-teachers once had a mishap during an English lesson. It was early one February and she noticed the calendar on the wall was still showing January so she went to tear the January page off only for the clock directly above the calendar to suddenly fall down, hit her and fracture her nose! Thankfully she made a good recovery.

teachers need alternative approaches. Above all, teachers should try and be as positive as possible.* When students show good attitude or do something well, they need openly praising in a sincere manner. Make sure it is obvious to the class what students are being praised for. Teachers should bring attention to the good students and take it away from students who are prone to making some kind of trouble or distraction in the classroom.†

Where possible, teachers should have very clear and visual rewards for students or groups doing well such as team points or individual stickers so that the other students can see the advantages and benefits of doing well and in turn strive to earn some of these rewards for themselves. Almost all students, including even those that often 'play up', ultimately do like to receive praise and good vibes from their teachers. Bear this in mind and try to positively reinforce the good things happening in the classroom as much as possible. In some cases the results may not be immediate but over time such positivity should reap rewards.

While I was qualifying as a primary school teacher in England, one of the buzz phrases was, 'Catch them being good' as opposed to catching and punishing students doing something undesirable or mischievous.

† This may, on occasions, include some tactical ignoring (see page 226) of certain kinds of minor misbehavior or lack of concentration to make sure the positive feeling being generated remains at the core of the classroom.

Private Tutoring

Private tutoring is a lucrative business in Korea with many parents spending a small fortune on extra classes for their offspring in a bid to boost their children's hopes of entering one of the best universities in the country. Most foreign teachers can expect to be approached at least once by parents or even co-workers with regards to tutoring and some will be asked on numerous occasions during their stay in Korea. There is a temptation to accept the offer (or even to go looking/advertising for students) as it could potentially offer a significant boost in income. However, it is important to always remember that for most foreign teachers in Korea, tutoring is illegal with potentially very serious consequences if caught, including heavy fines, temporary imprisonment or even deportation.

The majority of foreign teachers work on an E-2 Visa (see page 253). Tutoring on this visa is unacceptable in any shape or form. Foreign teachers who qualify for F-series visas either through marriage to a Korean or because they are Korean-American are able to do private tutoring in some situations but even then there are restrictions. They must get a license to do so, which will not be granted to certain teachers such as those working full-time in a public school. Depending on the region the foreign teacher lives in, the license may also specify a maximum that can be charged per hour. Naturally tax must also be paid on money earned from tutoring. These laws are not just limited to foreigners. Korean teachers must also get a license to tutor legally.

While some foreigners do choose to tutor, they take big risks. Threats of drastic punishments for those getting caught are not just there as a deterrent. They are real. While many may slip through the net, some foreigners do get caught. Stay safe. Don't do it!

Pronunciation

As is often the case when people learn a foreign language, Koreans sometimes struggle to pronounce certain English words. Words that often give them particular problems are those English words starting with the letter 'f'. This is because the Korean language does not have an 'f' sound. The nearest sound is a 'p' sound. This means that many Koreans often end up saying 'prog' instead of 'frog', 'pish' instead of 'fish', 'Prance' instead of 'France' amongst others.

Other problematic letters (for the same reasons) for Koreans are 'v' words, which they will sometimes pronounce with a 'b' sound ('video' often becomes 'bideo') and 'z' words, which they often pronounce with 'j' sounds ('zip' often becomes 'jip'). 'Th' sounds are also problematic. Unvoiced 'th' words such as 'think' often become 'sink' while voiced 'th' words such as 'that' become 'dat'. Finally, Koreans are prone to saying things such as 'Englishi' and 'orangji'. Teachers should show great patience and perseverance with students who mispronounce words. Ask students to look at your mouth carefully as you try to teach them how to say words correctly. Do not get frustrated with them as one of the main reasons for their errors is often the lack of equivalent sounds in their own language.

Punishment

There will almost certainly be times as a teacher when it feels like there is no other option but to punish or sanction one or more students. For a Korean teacher that may include corporal punishment (see page 135) but as already discussed, this is not an option for foreign teachers. Other popular Korean punishments include making the offending student(s) raise both arms straight up in the air for anything from a minute or so up to the best part of a lesson. Usually the students will be standing up or kneeling down while doing this although they may occasionally do it while remaining seated. Also squatting punishments get used where the students put one hand to each ear and squat up and down ten or twenty times or maybe more if the students are older or the teacher is particularly angry. Occasionally push-ups are also used. More western-style punishments used in Korea include making the 'problematic' students stand at the back of the classroom or in a corner (sometimes facing the wall), temporarily sending them out of the classroom* or not allowing them to go out of the classroom at break time or lunch time.

* It is rarely a good idea to send more than one student out of the classroom at once as they are quite likely to start playing around outside and perhaps even distract the students still in the classroom.

If a foreigner is co-teaching in a public school, the Korean teacher is usually supposed to be responsible for any punishments or classroom management issues. However, it is quite common for foreign teachers to also take steps to deal with students who are making trouble or not concentrating unless the Korean teacher specifically says not to or feels undermined. There are also many classes in public schools where foreigners teach alone (after-school classes, vacation classes or when the Korean teacher is unavailable or even simply does not turn up) and will have to take care of organizing the students. In an academy, the foreign teacher is almost always teaching alone and therefore always responsible for classroom management and any rewards or sanctions.

Before teaching for the first time, the foreign teacher should have some plans in place for how to punish students if needed. These plans should not include shouting extremely loudly at the students. Such action rarely has any long term benefits, not to mention risks possibly damaging the teacher's voice. Also avoid giving unscheduled or extra homework as a punishment as students will come to associate English homework and English tasks in general as a negative rather than a positive chance to consolidate, practise and develop what they have learned. Instead, making a student sit alone or at least next to someone away from close friends usually acts a reasonable deterrent.

As ever though, prevention remains better than cure and the use of seating plans to isolate certain students is usually a good method (see page 217), complemented by positive reinforcement (see page 202). A three strikes and out system is a common one with some teachers. If a student commits a minor transgression, consider writing the student's name on the board with a number three next to the name and then cross it out and write two. If the student does something else later on, cross the two out and write one. Finally if the student commits a third 'offence' cross the one out, write zero and sanction or punish the student. Usually the sight of a two next to their name will deter many students and keep them on their best behaviour for the rest of the class. Many students who do not heed the first warning, and see themselves later reduced to one point (i.e. last chance saloon) will finally fall into line. It offers them a clear and visual choice to correct their behaviour off their own back without the teacher having to scold them for every offence.

Once the three strikes system has been introduced to the students and they understand it, it often becomes unnecessary in subsequent lessons to even verbally point out to individuals that they have lost a chance. Even if they do not see the teacher quietly write their name and number of remaining chances on the board, their friends or a student seated next to them will often give them a bit of a prod to point out that they are living dangerously.

However, the best way of all to address and prevent behavioural issues is through good or excellent teaching which interests and excites all of the students to the extent that the teacher can stop thinking about the control of behaviour and focus almost exclusively on the management of learning. Teachers should be constantly asking themselves two questions. First, 'What do the students need to learn?' and secondly, 'How can that learning be made as interesting as possible?'

Q

Questions, Questions, Questions (2)

When a job offer is made to a prospective teacher, the recruiter (or workplace if applying directly) will almost inevitably say what a great school or academy it is and encourage a quick decision. Some recruiters will put pressure on by suggesting (usually falsely) that it may take a long time for another opportunity to present itself. Faced with such an important and potentially life-changing choice, it is vital to make a decision which is as well-informed as possible.

For most schools or academies, it is unlikely that a search on the internet will provide any information either positive or negative unless a school or academy has been blacklisted (and even if a search does provide some results, it may not necessarily be up-to-date or free from bias). The answer is to request contact with the teacher you will be replacing. If this request is refused for an academy job, that should set alarm bells ringing immediately and it is unlikely to be a good idea to take up the job offer. Most commonly an email address will be provided to contact the teacher and ask some questions. However, teachers applying for public school jobs will often only know their location and not the exact school until arriving in Korea, which means it will not be possible for the recruiter to provide a contact. This will make it more of a leap into the unknown but on the other hand, the risk is reduced by public schools generally being more reliable in fulfilling their contractual obligations.

It is important to ask about pay. Is it always paid on time each month? Are the reasons for any deductions clear? Have previous teachers always received their severance pay? Ask about your prospective accommodation. Is it comfortable, clean and not too old? Find out about the working conditions. How many hours will you teach per day/week? Are any additional demands made on your time at work? Are adequate teaching materials provided? Is the curriculum rigid or can teachers use some of their own ideas? Do the students study well/behave themselves? Is there support available if there are any major problems?

For public schools, also ask about co-teachers. Are they helpful and kind? Can they speak English well? What do they expect of their foreign teachers? Do they let foreign teachers take a full part in class? For academies, ask about the number of students and foreign teachers. How many students are in one class? Have the number of students been increasing or decreasing recently? Approximately how many students does the academy have in total? If the numbers have been decreasing and/or the total number of students is lower than fifty (and especially if the total is less than thirty), tread very carefully. If the numbers are dangerously low, the academy owner may suddenly have problems paying teacher salaries in full or in a worst-case scenario may even suddenly close the academy leaving the teacher in the lurch and probably without paying for the teacher's plane ticket home.

Finally, do not forget to ask outgoing teachers why they are leaving. If you get a reply but suddenly have more questions, do not be afraid to send a further email – after all it is a big decision and it is important to make the right choice. Most outgoing teachers will be happy to help you.

R

Recruiters

Many teachers use a recruiter to find a job in South Korea, especially if it is their first position in the country. Knowing which recruiters are good and which are not is a tricky business. Recruiters which attempt to charge a teacher for finding a job should be avoided. Most do not ask for money because they get paid by the school or academy they find the teacher for instead. Those who are pushy and try to suggest the job they offer is the only one that is likely to be available in the foreseeable future should be politely declined too. It is unusual but not unheard of for a contract clause stating that if the teacher wishes to leave early, he or she must refund the recruiter's fees. If presented with such a contract, give it a wide berth.

Better recruiters will have a well-maintained website and will respond to communication and questions promptly and courteously. Their email address will have a business-like feel to it. They will guide potential teachers through the process and assist with applying for a visa. Remember that when using a recruiter to find a job, you do not have to accept the first position offered if your gut feeling tells you not to. It is also worth bearing in mind that teachers are not forced to restrict themselves to applying with just one recruiter.

Re-entry Permit

Foreigners teaching in Korea may wish to take an overseas trip during a holiday at some point during their contract. If they do, they must get a single re-entry permit before leaving Korea. A multi re-entry permit is also available for those who will leave Korea more than once during the period their work visa covers. It is possible to get this from Incheon airport on the actual day of departing for a trip but this is not recommended as the time it takes could conceivably result in the applicant missing their flight, especially during busy times. It is much better for foreigners to get their re-entry permits in advance from their local immigration office.

Returning to Korea

One fact that is predominantly a positive reflection on Korea is the large amount of teachers who do one stint in the country and then return at a later date for another dose of Korean life and teaching. The reasons for returning vary enormously but common ones include the following; the first spell was very enjoyable and the teacher missed teaching and/or Korean life after returning home; the teacher always intended to go back to Korea quickly but just wanted an extended holiday between jobs (academy vacation time is usually very short and restricted); the teacher married a Korean!

It is also slightly surprising that even people who seemed to be negative or complaining about their work in Korea first time around sometimes end up returning (usually older and wiser). Possible reasons for these people returning include the following; unemployment back home; having a spell working back home and realizing that there is no such thing as a perfect job; they enjoyed Korean life the first time around but just got unlucky with their workplace or they worked in a public school and decide they want to give teaching in an academy a try or vice-versa.

Rote Learning

One common criticism of the Korean education system is about how much English study is set up to involve rote learning i.e. the memorization of huge amounts of vocabulary and grammar rules. Often Korean students (especially middle school and high school students) receive large word lists to learn on a weekly or even more frequent basis. Some of the words are words that English natives would rarely use in their lifetime! It is not very unusual for some older Koreans to understand English language grammar rules better than many English native speakers. However, this acquired knowledge comes at a cost. Students are often not taught how to apply this knowledge. Particularly this means they are unable to use or fully understand the vocabulary they learn in English conversations with foreigners.

The English speaking proficiency of the average Korean is often significantly below their reading or writing level, especially amongst older people. Therefore the importance of foreign English teachers is massive in Korea, to get the students more and more involved in actually speaking English in a variety of contexts, raising the confidence and fluency of Koreans and reducing their inhibitions.

S

Safe Searches

When a teacher is trying to explain the meaning of something to students, there will probably be occasions when the students cannot understand. In that situation drawing a picture is a common method to illustrate a vocabulary item. Another popular way is to show the students a picture from the internet, if there is a television or screen in the classroom to project computer images on. A little bit of caution is needed with this method though. There have been various anecdotes of teachers typing in a seemingly harmless word into the images search of major search engines only to be horrified for an undesirable image(s) or even pornographic image to appear amongst the results in front of the students.* And this too, despite having the filtering out of results containing adult images and videos on the strongest settings.

Prevent such problems using one of two methods. First, flick the screen off while doing a quick search and check that all results are suitable for the eyes of students before switching it back on. Second, use a Korean search engine instead of the leading western search engines. Most Korean computers will have a relevant page as the homepage. From there, type the vocabulary item in English

* Definitely not something a teacher wants the students to go home and tell their parents about!

in the rectangular box (labeled 검색 – this means search). This should bring a list of articles up as search results. Look for 이미지 (images) near the top of the page and click. The chances of any 'dodgy' images appearing on the screen are much smaller as Korean internet has stronger censorship than most western countries.

Same-Sex Schools

Many South Korean middle schools are single-sex schools. Although there are more mixed-sex middle schools than before there is a definite chance that a foreign teacher employed to work in a public school could end up at an all boys' or all girls' school.

Saturday

Public school contracts for foreign teachers clearly state that work is Monday to Friday with no Saturday work. The majority of foreigners working in academies and other places of English instruction also have Saturday and Sunday off although some contracts may have a foreigner working five days out of seven including weekends with days in the week off. This is generally the exception rather than the norm. Foreigners who sign contracts to teach adults are more likely to work at weekends than those teaching children. Make sure working days are clear before signing a contract. If a contract is asking you to work more than five days a week tread extremely carefully and strongly consider it to be a deal-breaker, unless the salary is very generous compared to regular contracts.

Although foreign public school teachers have no obligations to work on Saturdays, there may be rare occasions when the school organizes something on a Saturday and invites, suggests or even expects their foreign teacher to come along (this will vary from school to school and will not occur at all schools). Possible events may include hiking or other trips with the teachers or getting involved in sports days. Getting invited to weddings of co-workers and even their family members such as sons and daughters can become a fairly regular occurrence. If you want to go, that is great. You may be genuinely busy and unable to go, which schools should normally accept – it is not a workday for you after all. If you do not want to go, avoid flat refusals and make yourself seem genuinely busy.

Seating

In classrooms around the world, it is quite common for students whose attitudes towards study are not the best to congregate together at desks near the back of the room i.e. as far away from the teacher as possible. Korea is no different in this regard. Something for teachers to ponder is the use of seating plans, designating the same seat to students for each class, perhaps periodically making adjustments to keep things fresh such as a new seating plan each semester or every couple of months. This is particularly useful if the teacher already knows which students are least likely to concentrate in class and why.

Seating plans are common for public school classes

but less so for academies. There are many methods to arrange students including boy, girl, boy, girl or by level with any low level students getting placed next to someone with much higher ability and in a position to help the lower level student. Some students may be unimpressed or complain about being seated where the teacher wants them to sit, although the younger the student the less likely this is. Even if they do attempt to complain, the teacher should seat the students in an authoritative manner and not enter into negotiation.[*]

One possible option is to seat the students but give them a kind of get-out clause such as by declaring once they and the student they want to sit next to earn twenty-five or fifty points or stickers each they can change their seats and sit where they want. This strategy can be very effective in motivating the students to study well but be sure to set the bar high so that they have to show good attitude for several weeks or months even to reach the target number.

---

[*] Avoid the belief that students only fail to concentrate because they are 'naughty'. Sometimes they sit next to students that distract them or are a bad match. On other occasions, the work might be too easy or too difficult for them. They might even be bored due to the teacher creating 'dull' activities or not being inspiring enough. Addressing some of these issues can sometimes improve a situation dramatically.

Second Semester Blues

The Korean school year has two semesters. The first is March to August and the second is September to February. In public schools the students generally study better in the first semester. Their attitudes and behaviour often deteriorate as the second semester progresses, which sometimes makes it a challenging time for teachers.

Severance Pay

One of the nicest things about working in South Korea is an additional payment made to employees at the end of their one year contract. Severance pay (tweh-jik-gum 퇴직금), is sometimes described as a bonus but is actually a legal requirement. The payment is taxed. For most teachers, severance pay is essentially an extra month's salary paid after a twelve month contract. Teachers who earn different amounts each month will have their exact severance pay paid based on their average earnings for the last three months of their contract. Overtime is not taken into consideration.

Employees must work a whole year to qualify for severance pay. Even working one day less than a year would make a teacher ineligible. Severance pay is not paid pro-rata if working for less than a year.

Severance pay is a big burden to employers especially on top of airfares or travel allowances they are usually required to pay at the end of a foreign teacher's contract. On very rare occasions it brings out the worst in them as a small minority look for ways to avoid paying it. This has been known to include eleventh hour sackings (see page 153). In this situation help is available from the Labor Board (see page 170).

Six Month Contracts

When people first become interested in the idea of teaching English in Korea they often look at several job adverts and spot a common trend. Almost all contracts are twelve months long. Some people are daunted by the prospect of committing to the unknown for such a long time while others may want to spend a year enjoying new experiences but would perhaps prefer to spend a few months in Korea and a few months in one or more other countries. Hence a common question is, 'Is it possible to have a job with a six month contract in South Korea?' Generally, it is not possible for a first contract but subsequent contract renewals can be arranged for periods of less than one year, although most employers will prefer another one year commitment. Most contracts cannot be extended by more than a year at a time. People who really want to experience teaching in South Korea but absolutely cannot or do not want to commit for a year could consider summer or winter camps as a way of getting started in Korea (see page 129).

Sleepy Students

It is a tough life being a Korean student with school to attend in the day time and academies to attend in the evenings and even well into the night for many middle and high school students. Add homework and demanding, expectant parents on top of that and it becomes easy to understand why some students are quite sleepy in school.*

Sometimes native English teachers mention that a minority of their middle or high school students just want to sleep during class time. While this is unacceptable of course, understanding the reasons should help to tackle this problem more calmly if it occurs. Often, their indifference is unlikely to be a statement against the quality of the lessons taught by their foreign English instructors. More likely, it is a combination of their demanding life and perhaps also being turned off English by excessive exposure to rote learning (see page 214) of vocabulary and grammar by some of the Korean teachers who have taught them English.

Try to liven sleepy students up by ensuring classes are interesting with lots of activities which are neither too easy nor too difficult. If certain activities are not capturing their imagination, keep experimenting with new ones and mix classes up with pair work, group work and other ways of encouraging interaction.

---

* A good way to emphasize this is to quote the famous Korean saying, 'Sleep five hours and fail, sleep four hours and pass.'

Slippers!

Koreans never keep outdoor footwear on when they are at home and this usually extends to the workplace. While visitors to a school or company sometimes keep their shoes on, most Koreans take their shoes off as soon as they arrive at work and put on sandals or other kinds of soft slip-ons. Whatever they actually wear, Koreans collectively refer to all of these kinds of indoor wear as 'slippers'.*

Split Shifts

Most foreigners who accept jobs to teach adults English in Korea find themselves stuck with split shifts, working for perhaps three hours early in the morning and about three or four hours in the evenings i.e. before and after Koreans go to work. Some foreigners are drawn to these hours at first thinking it will give them a lot of time and freedom to enjoy themselves during the day and for some people this may be the case. However, the reality is often different as the foreign teacher sometimes finds such a schedule physically exhausting. Teachers considering accepting a contract involving split shifts should ponder the pros and cons carefully before signing.

Staring

One way which is often effective for getting the

---

* As a foreigner, it can feel rather odd at first to be wearing slippers with a suit or other smart clothes but you soon get used to it.

students concentration does not involve talking at all. If one or more students are talking when they should not be, one option is for the teacher to stand still and stare in their direction without saying anything. Continue staring until the students realize and for a couple of seconds after they have gone quiet again and are ready to pay full attention. If the students do not see the teacher staring at them, it is often still unnecessary for the teacher to speak as other students will point it out if the teacher stares long enough. It is a good way for a teacher to make a point without having to raise their voice. A particularly effective way of making a point is to actually stop in mid-sentence before starting the stare.

Strategic Positioning

Another useful non-verbal method of maintaining or regaining the attention of one or more noisy students is to move towards them once in a while and especially if they happen to be talking or messing around when they should not be. The sight of a teacher approaching them or standing next to them is often enough to quieten them down.

Student Rewards

When some people start out as teachers, whether it be as a student teacher or a foreigner teaching English, there is often a tendency to give the students lots of candy, chocolate or even small toys as rewards for being good for as little as a few minutes or for winning games. In some cases, these items may be offered in significant quantities by teachers that are having problems controlling the students' behavior or noise levels in the classroom in the hope that it will improve matters. However, in some cases it might inadvertently make matters worse. Teachers need to be careful to ensure they do not create situations whereby the students will only be good in class if they can see some sort of material reward on offer. It could get expensive!

On the other hand, if the teacher never offers anything to the students, it may be a battle to motivate them and keep them on side.* There are a massive number of systems that teachers use around the world, some of which are more effective than others. Instead of short-term delicious edible rewards, alternative and probably more effective incentives or reward schemes might include students collecting stickers, points or something similar over a significant period of time (keep it shorter in hagwons) as they show good attitude, contribute and

---

* Some teachers may consider it as bribery to offer rewards to students for doing things that one might expect them to be doing as a matter of course. This was the viewpoint I leaned towards when I started out, qualifying as a primary school teacher in England. One day, I discussed this with one of my mentor teachers and she gave me an interesting perspective, which after reflecting on it changed my way of thinking. She said, "It might help to think of it like this... Teachers get a salary for doing their job well so students should get something for doing their 'job' well."

participate well in class, help friends etc.

Some teachers use levels or stages. For instance, students might receive some classroom privileges, certificates[*], increased game time in the last lesson of the week or month, or maybe pencils or other items of stationery as they earn perhaps ten, twenty-five and then fifty stickers etc. The number of stickers or points can be adjusted as a teacher pleases. Another idea that sometimes works well in public elementary schools is to seat the students boy-girl, boy-girl at the beginning of a semester[†] and then allow them to switch seats to sit with their friends once both friends concerned have reached a set number of points or stickers. The number of stickers can be set at a particularly challenging amount so that the students have to do well for a long time, meaning that most students will not be able to change until the final few weeks of the term/semester.

---

[*] Using certificates (printed in colour and ideally laminated too) as a form of incentive is one of my favourites, even though it can become time-consuming. While they might not work for every teacher, I have used them successfully over many years and have seen the goal of earning one motivate many, many students in schools.

[†] Note that this is for public schools. Academy classes are much smaller and it is quite normal for students to sit where they want and change seats from lesson to lesson. Teachers should not be afraid to move noisier academy students though if they feel it will be beneficial.

T

Tactically Ignore

Some teachers attempt to respond to every little negative that happens in a classroom, rebuking any student for not paying total attention the whole time. Not only can this be physically and mentally demanding for a teacher, it may not always be the best way to approach matters, especially considering that it is totally unrealistic to expect all children to have perfect concentration the whole time when this task is even beyond adults.

Students play up in class for a whole number of reasons. They may be seated near too many of their close friends, which can affect their concentration, or conversely be next to someone they do not get on with at all. They may be finding their study too easy or too difficult or find a subject or teacher boring. They may have problems outside the classroom that pour over into the classroom. Some students may just be following the crowd if a few others are also causing some trouble. Sometimes though, they may just be seeking attention either from other students or from the teacher.

Some teachers seem to end up scolding the same student time after time, class after class. Despite this, the student in question does not change their behaviour. This is sometimes because the student enjoys or needs the attention, even if it comes in a negative form. This is where tactical ignoring can sometimes be effective.

If a student is causing a major disruption or bothering other students then it cannot usually be ignored. Certainly teachers should avoid allowing students to talk over them. On the other hand, if the student is just fidgeting, playing with small pieces of paper, just occasionally whispering into the ear of the next student or some other similar low level act of disruption or lack of attention it is *sometimes* better to choose to ignore it at least partially, especially if it is not bothering other students. If necessary it can be followed up with a quiet word in the student's ear later on or with praise when the student reverts to doing the right thing i.e. fully concentrating. If a student sees that certain negative actions are not going to provoke the teacher or become the centre of attention, he or she may well stop doing them or at least less often.

There are some clear benefits to clever and appropriate use of tactical ignoring. Not least is the fact that it allows lessons to flow and allows the teacher to facilitate student learning rather than getting bogged down with behavioural issues. However, it can be a difficult skill to use. It involves teachers making judgment calls, knowing when to ignore something and when not to. As with most things, it becomes easier with experience.

Teacher's Day

May 15th is Teacher's Day in South Korea. It is not a

holiday but it is still an important day. Students give presents as a token of their respect and gratitude to their teachers. Former students of a school sometimes visit their old school if their previous or favourite teacher(s) still work there, with carnations being the most common present.

Teaching Adults

The thought of teaching children and young learners does not appeal to everyone and there are also opportunities to teach English to adults in South Korea. Universities might fall into this category but there are additional possibilities. Some academies which focus mostly on children may offer a small number of classes for adults. There are however, a smaller number of academies which focus purely on teaching adults. Many may offer general English classes while some may also run Business English classes.

Due to the availability of adult students, work in this area may involve weekend classes or split shifts (see page 222). Classes will sometimes be very small. As with children, every adult learner is different so it is perhaps unfair to generalize but many adults will have a very clear motive for learning English and will often be highly motivated. This can make it very satisfying teaching them. It is also possible to get into very interesting conversations with them if their English is of a reasonable level. Those who are happy with their classes may occasionally show their appreciation by suggesting going out for a meal or something similar.

On the downside, adults often have higher (and on occasions unrealistic) expectations of rapid improvement. If they do not feel they are making the progress they want they may become disheartened and even quit their studies. Some Korean adults will have more fear of making mistakes than younger learners and may be reluctant to attempt speaking work. They will need the same encouragement, praise and support that children need. Some adults will have had English grammar rules drilled into them when they were at high school and despite fairly low speaking skills, they may actually have a better understanding of these rules than some inexperienced native English teachers. This can prompt some of them to ask teachers challenging questions. Teachers need to be very prepared.

Teaching Teachers

Many public schools ask their foreign teacher to teach an English class during school hours for the Korean teachers (or occasionally for the students' parents) for about one hour per week. Lots of foreign teachers worry about this class when they are first told about it and wonder what and how they should teach.

There is not necessarily a right way or a wrong way of teaching such a class. Some foreigners teach it much less formally than they would a regular students' class. If there are only a few teachers present, it should be acceptable for everyone to sit around a table with coffee or other drinks and proceed in a very relaxed environment.

Unless told differently, it is probably not necessary to ask each teacher to buy a textbook to work from. It may be better to find out what the teachers are interested in and generate class discussions around that. Using short quizzes or games during a class is also possible. If the teachers have reasonable English, trying to get one teacher to describe a word on a card for a partner to guess is a good speaking game, with wrong guesses not penalized and play continuing for as many words as possible during a set time such as one minute per teacher. Pairing teachers off and giving them other speaking activities or games to do can also be effective but think carefully about the activities as obviously teachers and children will not always enjoy the same style tasks.

Often these classes are introduced at the start of a school year with just a few teachers attending unless all staff have been ordered to attend by someone higher up such as the vice-principal. As the weeks progress, it is likely that the numbers will dwindle. Some weeks may not even have any teachers show up or may be cancelled in advance. This will not often be a direct reflection on the foreign teacher. It is more to do with the fact that the Korean teachers are usually very busy and when it comes down to it, learning English will not be the number one priority for them, especially if they find it difficult.

Telephone Teaching

A concept that is popular with some language academies is that of telephone teaching. It is popular with some academy owners as it is a way of trying to show the students' parents that the education fee is reaping some benefits as they hear their children speak some basic English on the telephone. It is also a useful skill for students to develop as even advanced speakers of foreign languages sometimes find it difficult to talk in their second language on the telephone.

Telephone teaching usually takes place at the end of the day after final class and is done by the foreign teacher(s) in academies. Selected students are phoned up at home and the foreign teacher then tries to engage them in simple English conversation on the telephone for just a few minutes (perhaps five minutes or less). Normally, it will just be a review of very recent class learning while it is fresh in the minds of students. It is unlikely to get more complicated than that as naturally if students cannot respond, their parents sitting nearby are not going to be impressed. Each student may get one call a week, with the academy working through all the students during the week.

Telephone teaching is far from universal and many foreign teachers in language academies may never have to do it. For those that do, it may sometimes fall into the category of least favourite duties but it should not prove unbearable. It is always worth bearing in mind that most jobs across all professions have at least one or two aspects that are less favourable than others.

TESOL Qualifications

Having a degree in any discipline is an essential qualification for obtaining the E-2 Visa. Additional qualifications related to teaching are not usually compulsory for getting a job in Korea although some public schools, academies or recruiters may state a preference for them when advertising. Some may give a slightly higher salary (usually about one hundred thousand won higher) to someone holding a TEFL or TESOL qualification (Teaching English to Speakers of Other Languages).

Many teachers wonder if they need TESOL or a similar qualification before starting out, especially if they have never taught before. While they are probably not worth doing just to get a slightly higher salary, most people will find they provide a sound foundation for a year teaching in Korea or even the beginning of a teaching career. Many teachers going into a classroom for the first time without any kind of relevant experience or training are likely to find the going challenging at times with no theoretical background or teaching techniques to fall back upon. Even experienced teachers have difficult classes or days from time to time.

Of course, TESOL courses cost money and many people may decide they are not worth it to teach for a year or two. Alternatively some people might decide to do a cheaper online version or a shorter one offered by their recruiter. While these kinds of courses may still provide a useful introduction to teaching, they are unlikely to be fully accredited (and thus ineligible for a salary increment) as full qualifications have several hours of observed classroom based teaching practice included in their assessment process. Additionally, those planning a career in teaching should note that such courses may not be recognized when applying for future jobs.

Some teachers who get a couple of years experience under their belts may look to take further qualifications to aid their professional development and boost their future employment prospects. Teachers in this situation who are looking to make a serious commitment could, amongst others, look into doing the Delta qualification (Diploma in Teaching English to Speakers of Other Languages) or a Masters Degree in Applied Linguistics.

The First Foreigner

On occasions, a foreigner may receive a job offer to teach somewhere which has never had a teacher from overseas before. It sounds like an intriguing proposition but is it a good one?

In the case of having an interview (usually by telephone) with the owner of an academy which has never employed a foreigner before, it would be useful to get a good feel of the owner's background. Consider asking whether he or she has lived in foreign countries before and for how long. Does he or she have any foreign friends in Korea? Try to grasp whether the owner has had much exposure to foreigners, particular from the west. Is the owner likely to have a reasonable grasp of western culture and how you think about things? (Of course it will not be a one way street though if you take a job there, as you should also be willing to try and understand how the owner thinks and how Korean customs and culture work.) The purpose of this is to try and establish whether you will be able to understand where each other come from, whether you will be able to get on cordially and avoid conflicts.

If the owner does not seem to have much experience of foreigners or can hardly speak English (this does happen), the foreigner has to make a judgment or go with gut feeling. Just because the owner is not used to foreigners does not mean you cannot be happy there, far from it. His or her character may be very good and the workplace and its system may be very strong.

Whether the owner does or does not have experience of English and foreigners, be sure to check there is an English syllabus in place and that the academy is prepared for their first native English teacher. Ask what books or materials you will have to use to teach. It does not matter if you have never heard the name of the book. The important point is that there *are* books ready to use. One of the last things an inexperienced foreigner needs is to turn up at an academy and get told they are in charge of making and putting a programme of study together!

After getting a feel for the owner and the place you are being asked to take a job at as the first ever foreigner, if you have any serious doubts you should almost certainly decline the job, even if you are going through a recruiter who is suggesting it is the only job currently available. The chances are that the recruiter will soon be back in touch with other job proposals that may feel more suitable. Even if that particular recruiter genuinely does not have other jobs at that time or refuses to help you find another job, there are plenty of other recruiters around.

In the case of public schools, a foreigner could end up being the first ever foreign teacher without being able to do anything about it as many foreigners sign contracts to work in a particular province and will not know which school they are going to until arriving in Korea. In this situation, some of the teachers should have other experience of foreigners, maybe at previous schools or through spells studying abroad or whatever. There should also be one or more Korean English teachers at the school who can make life more comfortable for the foreign teacher and hopefully get him or her integrating with the other teachers a bit, whether it be through school sporting events, dining out after work or whatever.

The Only Foreigner

Sometimes foreigners receive offers to go and teach at a school or academy where they will be the only foreign teacher. It is very frequent for them to wonder and ponder whether or not that will be a good thing. Some may deem it as daunting to be alone in a new country without any other foreigners immediately on hand and turn the offer down in the hope of getting another job where other foreigners do work.

The majority of foreigners working in public schools will be the only foreign teacher there. However, foreigners recruited through a major government sponsored programme and starting at one of the two regular times of the year (the beginning of March or September) will usually have a compulsory orientation, which offers the chance to meet and perhaps make friends with other foreigners who have just arrived in Korea. Some of these other new teachers will end up working in different cities or provinces though so there are no guarantees of building long-lasting friendships. There are other intermittent gatherings either just for those teachers within a particular province or for several provinces at once. Some are aimed at offering further training and developing teachers' skills more, while others are little more than brief socializing opportunities. Either way, there should be some chances to come into contact with other foreigners.

There are some English language academies which only employ one foreigner but most people who accept jobs to work in academies should end up with at least one other expat. Bigger academies may employ several foreigners, some of whom may end up becoming very close. Academies also tend to be concentrated very close together so there will probably be times when foreigners from different academies bump into each other, potentially offering the chance to build new acquaintances or friendships.

Foreigners working alone but living in cities should be able to meet other foreigners outside the workplace by joining local Korean classes, checking out bars or coffee shops that attract foreigners and so on. For those in more rural locations it might be more difficult but with an effort it should be possible to meet other foreigners, whether it be locally or by making the effort of travelling to nearby cities at the weekends.

So far this entry has been written on the assumption that foreigners would want at least some access to other foreigners to feel more at ease in an unfamiliar country but this is not always the case. Some people are happy to be alone and in their own company. Others may see it as a great opportunity to focus on building relationships with Korean people and perhaps attempt to learn Korean more quickly than the average foreigner. Some people end up being a lot more adventurous if they are a bit isolated and take more trips at weekends or vacations and explore more of Korea than those who always have fellow foreigners to turn to.

Another advantage of being the only foreigner teacher in a workplace is being more special. You might be the only foreigner the students have any real contact with. You will be an important part of each child's education. Also working with other foreigners does not guarantee happiness. There are often cases of foreign co-workers not hitting it off, having very little to do with each other outside of the workplace and building different friendships.

Disadvantages of being the only foreigner include not having anyone to immediately turn to, whether it be in relation to any workplace queries or issues that may arise or in terms of finding out information about expat life in the local community (where foreigners go at night, whether there are any English speaking doctors or dentists locally and where they are based, the best local bank to use when sending money home etc.). It can also be more challenging to make friends quickly and build a social life, which for some may be essential to settle in a new country and avoid any serious homesickness.

A final point worth exploring further when invited to work at an academy with no other foreign teacher is the issue of *why* there are no other foreigners. Is the academy quite new, starting to develop and genuinely heading in the right direction, especially in terms of student enrollment?

Did the academy use to have more than one foreign teacher and has shed its numbers either due to a falling number of students or to cut costs? How many students does the academy actually have?

If the academy has less than thirty students it might be very risky to accept a job there. Even less than fifty should see a prospective teacher tread very carefully. From those sorts of starting figures it only needs one sudden drop or exodus in the number of students the academy has to put it in extreme danger and perhaps at risk of closing down. If the academy did suddenly close, there is no guarantee that it would honour commitments such as buying the foreigner teacher a plane ticket back home. Before accepting a job as the only foreigner at an academy, try emailing the outgoing teacher to find out more related to the number of students and which way everything seems to be heading.

Timer

Teachers often give students a task and announce that the students have five, ten or fifteen minutes to finish the task only for the majority of the students to fail to complete the task within the time, thus needing more time potentially creating problems for the organization of the rest of the lesson. The teacher often ends up giving the students another two, three or five minutes at least once, and often on a further two or three occasions, and suddenly an activity takes double the time initially allocated for it.

There are various ways to try and ensure all or most students complete something within the teacher's desired time limit. Possibilities include offering a point or sticker (but try to avoid candy!) to the first few students or groups to complete the task. Perhaps more effective though is to have a computer timer counting down from five or ten minutes to zero that is very visible to the students i.e. on a screen or television in the classroom. The students can see how much time is left and generally work with more urgency.

The teacher should remind the students frequently about how many minutes are left. Nevertheless, this will not guarantee that all students finish within the time so a good tip is for teachers to decide in advance a time limit they are not prepared to exceed such as ten minutes and then allocate the time to the students in two steps (X + Y). For example give the students eight minutes, frequently reminding them of the time left to give them a hurry up. Then after the time has run out and a few students have still not finished, give them the final two minutes. These final two minutes should speed them up even more. A three step approach (such as 7 + 2 + 1) is also a possibility.

Total Physical Response

Often shortened to TPR, Total Physical Response is a teaching method used most commonly with beginner language learners, especially young children. The teacher gives spoken commands and the students must respond physically. There are a massive number of instructions a teacher can give such as, 'Stand up, sit down, jump, jump X times, touch your nose, pick up your pencil, stand next to your friend, turn around, look at X, clap your hands etc.' Simon Says is an example of a TPR game. Students list and follow commands, which may include, 'Simon says play tennis,' 'Simon says brush your teeth,' 'Simon says shake your friend's hand,' 'Simon says put your hands on your head' etc.

Many students are kinesthetic learners, meaning they learn best through movement so TPR activities can be very effective and enjoyable for these sorts of learners. Also many students will enjoy giving instructions to the rest of the class instead of the teacher so give some volunteers the chance to do so. As with other activities, avoid overusing it to ensure its motivating nature does not wear off.

Tourist Visa

Teaching (or tutoring) in Korea on a tourist visa is illegal in any shape or form. Do not trust an academy or school that says, 'There is no time to get a visa, come over now/start work now and we will send you on a visa run as soon as possible/on the first weekend you are here'. The consequences of teaching on a tourist visa can be dire. An unscrupulous employer could rip a foreign instructor off as he or she would have virtually no recourse if unpaid for work done, whether it be a week's work, a month or even longer. Worse still, if caught by the authorities, the foreigner is likely to be fined and deported.

Coming over on a tourist visa and *looking* for work is acceptable for foreigners who have worked in Korea before as long as they sort a visa out before actually starting work.* In some cases this is a good idea, as potential employers can be checked out face-to-face and the chances of landing a good school or academy to work at are higher. This can be an expensive way of doing things though with the requirement to pay for somewhere to stay while job-hunting. Also, reimbursement by a new employer of the airfare paid to travel to Korea is not always guaranteed in this situation because the foreigner is hired 'in-country'. Finally, note that airport immigration might not allow someone without a visa to enter with a one-way ticket. It is better to have a return ticket even if one half ultimately does not get used.

U

Unigwons

Unigwon is a word formed from university and hagwon and describes a job where the teacher works in a Korean university but teaches classes of children full-time

---

* Korea lets nationals from many countries enter for up to ninety days on a tourist visa but check in advance for up-to-date and country specific information.

rather than university students.* Generally pay is on the low side in unigwons but the number of holidays are usually at least as good if not better than public schools and significantly more than at hagwons. Check contracts carefully to see if other benefits such as plane tickets or airfare are included. Some teachers take a job at a unigwon in the hope that it will provide a foothold into the university when future jobs open up there teaching their university students. Whether this generally translates into reality is far from certain.

Universities

Many English teachers in Korea who stay beyond more than one year may aspire to work in a Korean university in the medium or long term. University teaching jobs are often held in high esteem and can be difficult to obtain. Unlike public schools and academies, they are often two year contracts offering more security. Many of these positions are very good indeed but as with public schools and academies some opportunities are better than others.

There are different kinds of university jobs. Some will be teaching conversational English classes. Others will be running credit bearing courses, which go towards the students' final grades. Sometimes foreign instructors teach

---

* As opposed to English camps at a university where the foreign instructor may be asked/told to teach some children's classes during school vacations but teaches university students for the rest of the year.

a subject other than English in which they have a strong academic background in (Masters Degree or PHD). This may be business studies, history or whatever. These courses are taught in English. Jobs as a conversational teacher will be the easiest to come by but competition will still be tough.

When universities advertize for new foreign instructors, they commonly state that they will only accept applications from holders of a Masters degree or above. Sometimes they will accept a Masters in any degree but it is common for them to specify a relevant degree such as one in linguistics or TESOL. Some universities may accept applications from teachers without a Masters but these universities are likely to be lower ranked, lower paid or rural based. Nevertheless these universities are often considered a good stepping stone towards working at a better university in the future.

Most universities look for applicants with experience, and the more relevant it is the better. Experience of teaching in Korea usually outweighs teaching experience anywhere else. Previous experience of working in a Korean university is one of the biggest plusses. The next step down is other teaching experience with adults and experience in Korean public high schools. Completed years in middle schools and elementary schools or academies might earn a bit of credit, especially if accompanied by good qualifications but experience teaching at high school level and above is preferred.

Applications from outside of Korea are possible even if the applicant has no previous experience of teaching in Korea but other than the most prestigious jobs where a PHD and a long list of publications are required, the chances of success are not great (although some have been successful over the years). Reasons for this include the fact that most universities will only interview face-to-face, which places those currently residing in Korea at a huge advantage. Also those that have been in Korea for some time may have built up some useful contacts perhaps including someone with influence at the university they apply to.[*]

Foreigners are attracted to Korean universities for a number of reasons. Some expect a more professional working environment or think it will be a better or more rewarding use of their skills and qualifications and perhaps more beneficial for their future career aspirations if they ever return to their home country. Others look forward to shorter teaching hours and longer vacations. Many may prefer to teach adults rather than kids. A minority may be attracted to the fact that they will most likely be called 'professor'.[†] Many do feel these rewards during their period

---

[*] This can have a massive bearing on who is employed. Who you know is so crucial in Korea.

[†] Most Korean universities use the word 'professor' differently to the west and some bestow the title of 'professor' on their lecturers even if their academic qualifications and experience do not merit it.

of employment at a university. In the best cases workloads may be as light as six to ten classes teaching a week with up to five months holiday per year! (Other duties may apply.) Others may have somewhere in the range of ten to about sixteen classes a week with two to three months annual vacation thrown in while university jobs at the bottom end may have teaching hours comparable to a public school and a similar or only marginally better holiday entitlement.

As with public school and academy jobs, university jobs often come with negatives. Disputes between Korean workers or superiors and foreign 'professors' do sometimes arise. Some may be under the assumption that university jobs are significantly better paid than public schools and academies but this is not always the case. At the top end they usually are and sometimes comfortably so, but at the bottom end they only pay similar or even lower salaries. Additionally some may not offer some of the benefits foreigners get elsewhere. For example plane tickets are not always provided at the end of the contract, or instead an amount of cash will be given that will not cover the total expense.

A house is sometimes not part of a university contract and only a housing allowance will be offered. In some cases, this will not be enough to cover the cost of renting. Class sizes can vary but are sometimes more than some teachers would consider suitable for conversational classes. Universities sometimes have a grading system whereby a certain number of students must get an A, another percentage must get a B and so on. Some foreign teachers are not comfortable with this. Student appraisals of each foreign teacher often play a part in whether the teacher is renewed. Some universities operate policies of limiting the number of times foreign teachers may renew their contracts, which is something that is not practiced at academies and public schools. The long vacations may be reduced by optional or compulsory camp classes (which can include periods of teaching children).* These will normally be compensated for with extra money so some will judge these camps positively while others will view them more negatively.

Many foreigners write or speak very positively of their experiences of working at Korean universities and suggest they could not imagine going back to working anywhere else in Korea. There are others that argue that the best public school jobs beat working in a university, especially if they provide good after-school class pay. Some people happily stay in academies for several years. Sometimes teachers have a strong preference for teaching children so the thought of applying to work in a university does not appeal to them. As ever, there is not a definite right or wrong path to take and each individual should take their own needs and happiness into account when choosing the best kind of workplace to work at or move on to.

---

* This is something worth checking prior to signing a contract.

V

Vacations

Korean people generally have very short vacations. Excluding national holidays and weekends, some Koreans may only get about two or three days tagged on either side of a weekend in the summer and then the same again in the winter. Foreigners teaching English in an academy often do not get much more than this. Approximately ten days paid holiday per year is normal although some do manage to get a little bit more than this (occasionally some foreigners ask for a bit extra *unpaid* for a short period between contracts although such requests may not always be granted). Some academies may want their teachers to take vacation when they say, rather than when the employee wants to use vacation, so check and double-check very carefully in advance, especially if planning expensive trips.

Foreign public school teachers usually get about twenty days regular vacation (give or take a day or two, depending on the province or school), with about two weeks during the school's summer vacation and two weeks during the winter vacation. An additional paid two weeks are given to teachers who renew their contracts. These two weeks are usually taken on weeks fifty-one and fifty-two of the contract and are designated as a time for visiting one's home country although the vacation can be used for other purposes such as trips elsewhere. Vacations are normally limited to these specified periods so that the foreign teacher is always available for regular semester time classes.

Requests for public school vacation at other time are unlikely to be granted, or often only on an unpaid basis. Schools may not appreciate such requests either. However, if there is a genuinely good reason for needing a short vacation at another time such as the wedding of a sibling or a grandparent's one hundredth birthday celebration, it may be worth trying. Foreigners who know which school they will be working at in advance, or are renewing contracts should consider trying to get vacation outside of normal times authorized in advance of signing their contract.

Some public schools may give their foreign teacher more vacation time than the regular four weeks or so.* This can happen anywhere, although it tends to happen more at smaller rural schools. This additional vacation may be stated in the contract but often will not be and should therefore be treated as a bonus. This used to happen a lot more previously than it does now. The main reason for this is that some of those with the extra vacation went around boasting about it and those who only had regular vacation (and especially those doing a lot of deskwarming – see page 149) became upset about it and some complained. Rather than increasing vacation for everyone to even things up,

* This might just be a couple of days but can sometimes be several weeks extra. I have had a couple of friends in the public school system who got as many as ten weeks a year off.

those in authority sent instructions to try and ensure schools did not give any bonus vacation to anyone, thus taking away the privilege from many of those that were getting it. These instructions also seem to get re-circulated every once in a while to remind schools. However, some schools do continue to give some extra time so if you are one of the lucky ones, keep it quiet or you too could find yourself losing your little perk in a further crackdown.

Visa Run

Sometimes a foreign English teacher comes to Korea without a job, entering as a tourist and then finds employment after a period of job hunting. Alternatively, a teacher may leave one job mid-contract and then find another one without leaving the country (subject to receiving a letter of release – see page 179). In either case, the teacher needs a brand new visa before commencing work, otherwise he or she would be working illegally. This visa cannot be obtained within Korea so the teacher is required to do a visa run. This means leaving Korea and going to a Korean embassy elsewhere to get the visa and then returning, usually about two days later. While other locations are possible, Fukuoka in Japan tends to be the most popular place to go on a visa run either by ferry from Busan or by plane from Incheon.

Volleyball

It is very common for public school teachers to get together at least once a week to play volleyball. This will often take place during school time. Several of the Korean teachers will often be good players as it is a fairly popular sport in Korea. If you take a job in a public school, you may well get asked whether you wish to participate (in some cases you may well be told to join in, rather than being asked). If you like volleyball or are good at it then great, but even if you are hopeless at volleyball or have never played, it is likely to please your co-workers if you join in. If your ability is low, you may quickly find yourself placed somewhere near the back of the court where the ball is unlikely to come to you very often. That may sound like a perfect arrangement or it could seem like a recipe for boredom. Even if this does not sound like much fun, you could grin and bear it and try and get into the spirit of things, joining in with the high fives after your team wins a point, and doing the best that you can when the ball does actually come to you, or when it is your turn to serve.

If you decide not to, or would prefer not to get involved with volleyball, you could stress how little it is played in your own country, hope your co-workers understand and then demonstrate your full support for the school by watching enthusiastically if they ever have matches against other schools. It is worth remembering the fact that being part of the group is such a very important aspect of Korean society.

Why?

Many new teachers may talk to their students well but make the mistake of asking too many closed questions for which, the students can only give one word answers. While they may improve their listening skills being exposed to these kinds of questions, it is not going to help them practice their speaking skills much. Teachers should try to ask more open-ended questions, or if a student answers a question with only a one word answer, try to probe them further asking, 'Why?' as often as possible. Depending on their level and the complexity of the subject being discussed, some students will be able to expand their answers well while others may not be able to get past the one word answer but by challenging them a bit and taking them out of their comfort zone sometimes, the results should come little by little. It is a good feeling watching and listening as students, sometimes confidently and in other cases with great trepidation, manage to go past the one word answer stage and progress to constructing short sentences and beyond.

Work Clothes

As you would expect, teachers dress very professionally in public schools. Schools will expect high standards of attire from their foreign teachers too. Males should wear a suit, or at the very least a shirt and tie. It will normally be okay to remove the tie when it is hot. In the winter it is usually fine to wear thicker tops rather than a shirt and tie as long they look smart. Female teachers do not need suits but should obviously dress smartly.

Academies tend to be less formal and smart casual will normally be acceptable. Sometimes, even a very casual look will suffice but this may vary from academy to academy. If they are having a special day or event, it might be necessary to dress up much smarter so even foreigners who go to Korea to work in an academy should take at least one suit, even if it might not end up getting used often.

Work Visa

Teaching on a tourist visa is illegal in Korea so most foreign English teachers need to apply for and receive an E-2 work visa before coming to South Korea.* Only teachers from America, Canada, United Kingdom, Ireland, Australia, New Zealand and South Africa are eligible for an E-2 visa and they must have a degree certificate. Applications must go to the Korean embassy in one's home country. Requirements get tweaked from time to time but usually consist of the following; a copy of the teacher's degree certificate notarized with an apostille, health check, criminal check covering the whole country the teacher is from, university transcripts, an employment contract and passport photos. Many applicants will also be interviewed at their nearest Korean embassy. Recruiters will guide applicants through the process and additional information

---

* Exceptions are some university instructors who will need an E-1 visa and international school teachers who will usually need an E-7 visa.

and details of documents required can also be obtained from a local Korean embassy. *It is very important to check the latest requirements as changes are made periodically and sometimes at short notice.*

Native English teachers who are married to a Korean and Korean-Americans are usually able to apply for F series visas which give additional rights. Different documents are required for these visas so check at the time of application. A teacher starting out on an E-2 visa who then goes on to marry a Korean may apply for an F series visa at that point.

Worst-Case Scenario

An essential piece of advice for foreigners heading off to teach English in Korea is to be prepared. Particularly, this means taking an adequate amount of money and having a credit card with a reasonable limit or immediate access to other sources of money just in case. Thankfully worst-case scenarios are the exception not the norm but things do sometimes go wrong.

Your workplace will have promised to refund your plane ticket or pay an entry allowance soon after arriving in Korea (in rare cases, they may even buy your ticket for you before you travel). If this money is not forthcoming within a reasonable time frame (ideally with the first month's pay at the very, very latest but usually much sooner) and a whole host of other promises are broken early on, or even worse there are signs of illegal activity going on, the foreigner worker may feel it is necessary to take drastic measures. Possible courses of action include leaving immediately, either by handing in their notice virtually straightaway or even more dramatically just 'disappearing' i.e. getting on the first plane back home. This is known amongst foreigners in Korea as doing a 'Midnight Runner' (see page 180). *

However, before even contemplating such extreme courses of action, foreigners having any big problems should get in contact with the recruiter who placed them with a particular school or academy to see whether the recruiter can mediate or solve the problem one way or another. If there are other teachers in the academy or school, they might be able to help too. Also bear in mind that if you leave a job quickly but do wish to take another job in Korea in the future, it could make it more difficult (but probably not impossible) for you to find employment later on.

Prevention is better than cure and being prepared also means doing your homework before signing a contract to teach in Korea. There are several useful and important

---

* That is certainly not a course of action I would wish to condone although having never been in that situation myself and having never seen other foreigners I know experience it either, it is difficult to pass judgment.

questions (see page 209) you should ask other foreign workers currently employed at the workplace you are considering, to get a good picture of your potential place of employment. You can also type the workplace into an internet search engine to see if anything turns up. While there are no guarantees, if you do your homework, the odds of finding a good or at least reasonable workplace are in your favour. All things considered, most people do have positive experiences in Korea.

'You're the Teacher!'

Some teachers monopolize classrooms and lessons and totally control classes from the front, often talking for too long and not giving students enough chances to practice the learning goals of a given lesson. One way of addressing or preventing that is to appoint a student volunteer to temporarily take over the teacher role. This is often very popular with young elementary school children and makes lessons much more student-centred.

First of all, the classroom teacher introduces key vocabulary, a target question, selection of answers or other sentence structure and then works through some examples with the students. As students increase in confidence, volunteers can then assume the teacher role. Choose students in turn to become a teacher (actually call them a 'teacher' instead of saying something like, 'Who wants to come to the front?') and allow them to ask questions to about three other students, with the children teachers choosing who can answer their questions. The regular classroom teacher steps back and just facilitates while trying to ensure that as many students as possible are being involved in the lesson.

After a few students have had the chance to be a teacher in front of the whole class, put the students into small groups and practice the activity in their groups (providing suitable resources such as picture cards as needed). The classroom teacher chooses who will be the 'teacher' first in each group and gives them time to ask target questions for other students in their group to answer. The teacher then keeps changing who the teacher is in each group about every couple of minutes, trying to ensure that every student has a chance to be the teacher once.

Appendices

Appendix One

Summary of Hagwons

Main Pros

- Small class sizes.
- More likely to work with other foreign teachers.
- The Korean teachers are more likely to speak good English.
- A good place to begin to develop teaching skills.
- Foreign teachers always teach alone, allowing more freedom to organise lessons as they please.

Main Cons

- A minority are unreliable for paying salary promptly and in full plus other contractual obligations such as severance pay and pensions.
- They are run like businesses. Owners want to keep students and thus may not take steps to deal with any extremely unruly children.
- Holiday allowance is usually less than at public schools. Workers sometimes have to take their holidays when their employer says.

Appendix Two

Summary of Public Schools

Main Pros

- Usually provide a full induction programme if hired during regular recruitment cycles.
- Increased stability. Rarely any problems with contractual obligations.
- Some may offer extra after-school classes which can offer the chance to significantly boost the teacher's salary.
- Teachers generally receive more respect than at academies.
- Usually have longer vacation than academies.

Main Cons

- Larger class sizes.
- In some cases, foreign teachers may have to work at more than one school.
- Some foreign teachers have co-teacher issues.
- Some foreign teachers do not enjoy after school dinners and other socialising with the Korean school teachers, which depending on the school may be virtually obligatory.

Appendix Three

International Schools in South Korea

The number of international schools providing a western education for expat children in South Korea is rapidly expanding and the following list is intended as a sample of the available schools around the country rather than a complete and definitive list.

- Dulwich College, Seoul
- Korea International School
- Busan Foreign School
- Okpo International School
- Lycee Francais de Seoul
- Gyeonggi Suwon International School
- Gyeongnam International Foreign School
- Deutsche Schule Seoul
- Taejon Christian International School
- British School of Seoul Foreign School
- Daegu International School
- Gwangju Foreign School

Appendix Four

An Introduction to Different Types of Korean Hospitals

내과 nae-gwa	(Internal Treatment)
안과 an-gwa	(Eyes)
이비인후과 e-bee-in-hu-gwa	(Ears, Nose and Throat)
외과 weh-gwa	(General Surgery)
피부과 pee-bu-gwa	(Dermatology)
치과 chi-gwa	(Dentist)
산부인과 san-bu-in-gwa	(Maternity)
소아과 so-ah-gwa	(Pediatrics)
한의원 han-uee-won	(Oriental Medicine)
성형외과 seong-hyeong-weh-gwa	(Plastic Surgery)

Appendix Five

A selection of spelling differences between British English and American English

The American English variations are in brackets.

our/or

colour (color), favourite (favorite), humour (humor)

re/er

centre (center), litre (liter), metre (meter), theatre (theater)

se/ze

apologise (apologize), organise(organize)

gue/g

catalogue (catalog), dialogue (dialog)

ce/se

defence (defense), licence - noun (license)

others

programme (program), grey (gray), tyre (tire)

Appendix Six

A selection of differences in vocabulary between British English and American English

The following list is sorted by approximate frequency of usage in an English as a Foreign Language classroom with the most used vocabulary first. The American English variations of each word are in brackets:

sweets (candy), mum (mom), holiday (vacation)

rubber (eraser), maths (math), toilet (restroom)

trousers (pants), trainers (sneakers), film (movie)

cinema (movie theatre), crisps (chips) bath (bath tub)

head teacher (principal), postman (mail carrier)

car park (parking lot), chemist (drug store)

ice lolly (popsicle), underground/tube (subway)

torch (flashlight), petrol (gas), nappy (diaper)

About the author

Adrian Bozon is a qualified England primary school teacher. He has also taught English as a Foreign Language to students of all ages, most notably for several years in a South Korean elementary school as well as an earlier spell working in a hagwon. He has taught students of all ability levels in small, medium and large class sizes. He has taught in various teaching environments including extensive experience of team-teaching in addition to regular solo-teaching. Adrian has also worked closely with over two hundred Korean student teachers.

Also by Adrian Bozon

100 Great EFL Games: Exciting Language Games for Young Learners (ISBN: 978-0956796806)

100 Great EFL Quizzes, Puzzles and Challenges: Stimulating, Photocopiable, Language Activities for Teaching English to Children and Young Learners of ESL and EFL (ISBN: 978-0956796813)

100 Great EFL Quizzes, Puzzles and Challenges Volume Two: Photocopiable, Activities for Teaching English to Children and Young Learners of ESL and EFL (ISBN: 978-0956796820)

Lightning Source UK Ltd.
Milton Keynes UK
UKOW032253150113

204896UK00009B/781/P

9 780956 796837